THE PATRIOTS

THE
PATRIOTS

THE AMERICAN REVOLUTION
GENERATION OF GENIUS

EDITED BY VIRGINIUS DABNEY
INTRODUCTION BY
HENRY STEELE COMMAGER

New York

ATHENEUM

THE U.S. BICENTENNIAL SOCIETY

The U.S. Bicentennial Society, headquartered in Richmond, Virginia, is a private, non-governmental organization formed by a group of distinguished Americans to commemorate the nation's 200th anniversary.

The Society is marking the bicentennial by authorizing the issuance of tasteful objects of artistic and historic significance related to the history of the United States.

The Society has adopted as its hallmark the "Double Eagle"— two eagles with spread wings, standing on olive branches and representing the two centuries since the United States was founded. One eagle looks proudly to the past, the other confidently to the future.

copy 1

Copyright © 1975 by The U.S. Bicentennial Society
All rights reserved
Library of Congress catalog card number 75–13801
ISBN *0–689–10690–4*
Published simultaneously in Canada by McClelland and Stewart Ltd
Typesetting and preliminary text printing by Connecticut Printers Inc.,
Hartford, Connecticut
Illustrations and accompanying text printing by
Rapoport Printing Corporation, New York
Bound by H. Wolff, New York
Designed by Harry Ford
First Edition

FOREWORD

THE FIFTY PATRIOTS of the American Revolution whose careers are briefly sketched in this volume are all worthy of remembrance. We do not pretend to say, of course, that every significant revolutionary leader is included, but rather that each of the men and women in the pages that follow made a memorable and important contribution to the establishment of the republic.

A few were not actually involved in the revolutionary war itself, but are recognized here as founders of American culture, and hence deserving of our tribute.

We venture to assert that the list of authors assembled for this volume is one of the most distinguished ever put together within the covers of a single book. The assessments that these eminent historians have given of this astounding group of men and women should be of lasting value. We know of nothing quite comparable to it. The contributors have presented each of their subjects in their own individual styles, with no attempt on our part to impose uniformity.

Each patriot is considered here within the compass of from five to seven hundred words. We are grateful to numerous museums, galleries, and private collections for making available the fine portrait illustrations.

Highlights of each career are touched upon in the brief essays. Those wishing to study any of the subjects in greater depth can do so with our profile as a point of departure.

Three women have been included as typifying the patriotism and courage of their sex during those perilous years.

The omission of certain popular heroes and heroines will doubtless be noted. Among these are Paul Revere, Betsy Ross, and Molly Pitcher.

Revere was not included because although he was an ardent patriot, who took part in the Boston Tea Party and other such manifestations, his "midnight ride" was of little or no importance, despite the fantastic assertions of the poet Longfellow. The latter declared that "the fate of a nation was riding that night" in the person of Paul Revere. The facts are that Revere was captured by the British before he got to Concord, and that the warning he gave at Lexington could just as well have been given by William Dawes, who arrived half an hour behind him. Furthermore, the Americans saw the signal in the tower of the Old North Church, warning them as to the coming of the British, before Revere so much as mounted his steed. All this is set forth in Esther Forbes's authoritative book *Paul Revere and the World He Lived In* as well as in other works on the subject. Longfellow has perpetuated a myth that apparently will never die.

On top of all else, Paul Revere was a leading participant in the disastrous Penobscot expedition of 1779. In that memorable fiasco, the Americans fled headlong before a much smaller British force. Lieutenant-Colonel Revere and others were court-martialed, and he received an acquittal "with equal honor as the other officers in the same expedition."

So Revere was not the transcendent hero that many have thought him to be. He did risk his life, and was one of the early agitators for independence. He was also a fine silversmith and a versatile craftsman in several other directions.

Betsy Ross is left out of *The Patriots* because there is no convincing evidence that she either designed or sewed the first Stars and Stripes.

Molly Pitcher did indeed bring pitchers of water to the wounded at the Battle of Monmouth, and then helped to serve the guns herself when her husband was overcome by the heat. Yet this admirable exploit hardly qualifies her to be listed among our fifty American patriots.

Dr. Henry Steele Commager's comprehensive introduction to the present work places the entire Revolutionary Era magnificently in perspective. His able analysis will serve to open the eyes of many to the significance of our forefathers' achievements during those stirring years.

It is our hope that this volume will bring to Americans a greater realization of the meaning of the Revolution, and that it will help all of us to rededicate ourselves to the principles on which our country was founded.

The courage and tenacity of George Washington, the brilliance and versatility of Benjamin Franklin and Thomas Jefferson, the fiery patriotism of Samuel Adams, James Otis and Patrick Henry, the gifted pen of Mercy Warren, and the sacrificial heroism of Nathan Hale, all serve to inspire us today. Let us take to heart the brave deeds of these valiant men and women, who two hundred years ago offered their lives and fortunes in the cause of liberty.

It is apparent that we are the beneficiaries of an unparalleled generation of genius. To this genius *The Patriots* is dedicated.

Virginius Dabney

CONTENTS

CONTENTS

ILLUSTRATIONS

COLOR PLATES

[ix]

ILLUSTRATIONS

MONOCHROME PLATES

ILLUSTRATIONS

ILLUSTRATIONS

THE PATRIOTS

Henry Steele Commager

REVOLUTION AND ENLIGHTENMENT

AMERICANS BEGIN A NEW ERA

WE CELEBRATE, in 1976, the formal separation of the American colonies from the mother country, and the creation of an independent United States. That celebration inevitably conjures up a host of memories and associations: the minutemen who stood at Concord Bridge and "fired the shot heard round the world"; Joseph Warren dead at Breed's Hill, which later generations were to remember as Bunker Hill; Ethan Allen invoking "Jehovah and the Continental Congress" before Ticonderoga; John Paul Jones announcing aboard the *Serapis*, "We have just begun to fight"; Washington crossing the Delaware; Tom Paine writing the *Crisis* papers by the flickering light of camp fires; ragged Continentals somehow surviving the bitter winter at Valley Forge; Green Mountain Boys rallying at Bennington to turn back German mercenaries in redcoats; George Rogers Clark wading the swollen waters of the Wabash to capture Vincennes; John Morgan driving Tarleton at Cowpens; "The World Turned Upside Down" at Yorktown; Washington pleading with his officers at Newburgh, "You will, by the dignity of your conduct, afford occasion for posterity to say when speaking of the glorious example you have exhibited, had this day been wanting the world would never have seen the last stage of perfection to which human nature is capable of attaining."

It is all part of a great drama, one guaranteed to stir the memories, to excite the passions, to inspire the imaginations of Americans conscious of their heritage.

[3]

But while all these, and hundreds of comparable episodes in the drama of the war contributed to, and were essential to, the Revolution, they were not the Revolution. For the Revolution was not primarily the dissolution of an old empire but the creation of a new empire, one which was not only territorial but, in the familiar phrase of the day, "an Empire of Reason." It was not merely the repudiation of a royal sovereignty but—for the first time in history—the triumph of popular sovereignty. For the American Revolution was, politically, the most creative chapter in the whole of modern history. It is this creative quality that makes the American Revolution not merely an American but a world event. It had an immediate impact on France, on the many states of Latin America, on the peoples of Italy, of Greece, of Spain, even of England, where Tom Paine himself tried to bring about a revolution on American lines. All through the nineteenth century and even into the twentieth it worked like a ferment on the peoples of the Old World and of more distant continents, and its influence still quickens the political imagination of men and women in every quarter of the globe.

The Founding Fathers themselves were ever conscious of a role that history had thrust upon them, and of a mission that they felt called upon to fulfill. Never was there a more history-minded generation, history-minded for the past and for the future alike; for they were as conscious of their obligation to posterity as they were of their debt to the past. They were familiar enough with that past—especially its classical lineaments—and with the "lessons" that the past imposed upon them. They knew that history was philosophy teaching by examples (the phrase is from the much-admired Lord Bolingbroke), and most of them agreed on the examples that were relevant and on the lessons that these taught. Yet few of them were prepared to accept the conclusion that America was inexorably bound by the past or subject to its moral lessons. For most of them concluded that while the New World was not exempt from history, neither was it the prisoner of history; it was to be the special providence of America to launch a new era in history, and to embark upon a series of experiments that had no precedents in the past of mankind.

A NEW-FOUND EDEN?

H E R E in this New World, which was in the eyes of so many of the philosophes a new-found Eden, man was to have a second chance. Here in this great historical laboratory it might be possible to work out new laws of history, not so much for the past as for the future. Here might be traced the interaction between heredity and environment—the inheritance not of Britain or of Europe alone, but of all civilization; for America was to be the heir of all civilization; the environment richer, and more varied, than any that had so far been vouchsafed mankind.

Here, too, it would be possible to discover whether man was indeed capable of governing himself; whether government could solve that most intractable of all problems, the reconciliation of liberty and order; and whether man, if free, could vindicate his freedom in the moral, as in the political and social, arena. Here it might be possible to create a civilization rich not only materially, but culturally and ethically; one that would be prosperous, free, and just. Here, in circumstances that seemed ideal, men could work out their destinies free from those tyrannies which had plagued them from the beginning of time: the tyranny of the conqueror, of the despot, of the state; the tyranny of the priest and the church; the tyranny of ignorance and poverty, plague and war. Here, for the first time since the expulsion from Eden, man might be what God and Nature intended him to be!

For Washington and Franklin, for Jefferson and Tom Paine, and for a host of their co-revolutionaries, the American people now had an opportunity to triumph over the past and to mold the future. That was what Washington meant when he wrote in his Circular Letter to the States in 1783, that "The Foundation of our empire was not laid in the gloomy age of ignorance and superstition, but an epoch when the rights of mankind were better understood and more clearly defined than at any former period, the researches of the human mind after social happiness carried to a greater extent, and the treasures of knowledge, acquired by the labours of philosophers, sages and legislatures, laid open for our use." That is what Jefferson meant when he wrote of America that "this whole chapter in the history of man is new. The great extent of our territory is new. The mighty wave of public opinion which has rolled over it is new." That is what the French statesman Turgot meant when he wrote of Americans that "This people is the hope of the human race." Perhaps Tom Paine put it more dramatically than anyone—he had, after all, a certain genius for drama: the American, he said, was a new Adam in a new Paradise.

All the auspices were favorable, all but the hateful institution of slavery, and most of the Founding Fathers were confident that the new nation would soon rid itself of that curse. Americans occupied the most extensive territory of any western nation (we sometimes forget that America was born the largest nation in the western world), and the richest, too. There was land enough, said Jefferson in his wonderful first inaugural address, "for our descendants to the thousandth and thousandth generation"—and this at a time when the Mississippi River was the western boundary of the nation. The Americans possessed a "benign government" that did not "take from the mouth of labour the bread it has earned" (it is, of course, Jefferson again); they enjoyed geographical isolation and hence immunity from the wars of one-quarter of the globe and "the degradations" of the others, and they could, so they thought, look forward with confidence to centuries of peace.

[5]

They boasted religious freedom, and freedom, too, from those religious antipathies and wars that had made a shambles of so many Old World societies. They were an enlightened people, with standards of literacy as high as any in the world, and so committed were they to education that even during the years of war and turmoil they managed to double the number of their colleges—from nine to eighteen, no less—and to lay the foundations for a system of publicly supported education in the great Northwest—a system which spread, eventually, throughout the Republic. They cherished science (they called it natural philosophy) and made important contributions to it, and they made the benefits of their scientific studies available to all men who were free, for they displayed early that talent for the practical in science which was to distinguish them for another two centuries. Thanks to a century and a half experience in self-government (in some states, anyway) they were more mature politically than any other people on earth, and more creative, too.

It is that creativity that impresses us most, perhaps because we are so hopelessly unable to emulate it today. The creativity was, to be sure, chiefly institutional. Americans did not originate the ideas that Thomas Jefferson set forth with such matchless eloquence—and such matchless succinctness, too—in the preamble of the Declaration: that all men are created equal, that they are endowed by God and Nature with unalienable rights, that among these rights are life, liberty, and the pursuit of happiness, and that, as government derives all its powers from the consent of the governed, it is the purpose of government to secure these rights. There was some truth in John Adams's ill-natured remark that there was not an idea in the Declaration that had not been hackneyed about for years: he might well have said for centuries. But as Jefferson himself observed, it was not his purpose to justify independence on principles that no one had ever heard of before. To a generation trained on the classics of Greece and Rome and familiar with the philosophy that had animated the Commonwealthmen of the seventeenth, and the eighteenth, century, they were, in the happy phrase of Tom Paine's, the common sense of the matter. They were rooted in history; even better (so Jefferson and his colleagues believed) they were rooted in reason. They were part of the moral inheritance of western man; they were at the same time demonstrably vindicated by the laws of nature and nature's God. For the Founding Fathers (John Adams, to be sure, with some reservations for others, though not for himself) accepted unquestioningly the axiom that Reason was sovereign, that it could penetrate to and master the laws of nature and could persuade men and governments to conform to them. Looking back over half a century the aged Jefferson selected this as the animating principle of his age:

> We believed that man was a rational animal. . . . We believed that men, habituated to thinking for themselves, and to follow their reason as guide, would be more easily and safely governed than with minds nourished in error and vitiated and debased by ignorance.

Much of this was commonplace in the era of the Enlightenment—commonplace among the philosophes of Paris, or at the courts of Frederick the Great or Catherine of Russia or Gustavus of Sweden, among the Academicians of the Italian states, members of the Royal Society in London or the universities in Scotland. What was not commonplace—what was, indeed, unique, was the situation in America. For alone of all the peoples who embraced the Enlightenment, the Americans "*realized* the theories of the wisest writers," and transformed philosophical ideas into institutions that worked.

Those institutions embraced almost the whole world of government and politics, and not politics alone, but social and economic and cultural institutions as well. It is sobering to reflect that every major American political institution was invented or contrived before 1800, and that not one has been invented or contrived since, and that the great principles of social philosophy to which we seek to conform, are rooted, too, in the thought and the institutions of the revolutionary era.

Let us contemplate some of these political, constitutional, and social innovations.

THEY CREATED A NATION

F I R S T, the Founding Fathers created a *nation*—"brought forth," in Lincoln's phrase—something no people had ever done before; heretofore nations had not been "created" but had simply grown. John Adams put the matter well in his famous letter to Hezekiah Niles of *Register* fame: "Thirteen clocks were made to strike together, a perfection of mechanism which no artist had ever before effected." There were discords as well as chords, to be sure, but in the face of all experience and all predictions the new and artificially created nation survived, and survived, what is more, as a republic. That was something the magisterial Montesquieu and his followers had said was impossible, for it was taken for granted that republican government was suitable only to very small nations: an Athens, a youthful Rome, a Genoa, a Venice, a Holland; but a nation as large territorially as the new United States (born the largest nation in the western world) had no choice but that of despotism! It survived, too, without those familiar stigmata of nationalism in the Old World: a monarch, a capital, a ruling class, an established church, an army and a navy; and without that body of history, tradition, heroes, and legends assumed to be essential to the creation of national unity and loyalty.

Most of these, Americans did not want. Certainly they did not want a monarch or a ruling class or an established church, and they devoted their talents to getting rid of them. What they did want was, no doubt, history, traditions, and heroes, and these they managed to acquire with ease. They were fortunate, above all, in their heroes: Washington was a legend even in his lifetime; as John Adams said, he made every crowned head in Europe look like a valet. Noble, incorruptible, Olympian, courageous in war, sagacious in peace, he was such a father as every country desired and no other had: not mythical like Remus or Romulus, like Horsa or Hengist, like Hoger Danske or Barbarossa, but a man known to all and revered by all; how easy it was to accept Parson Weems's portrait of him as a paragon of all virtues, the admiration and envy of the world and of Heaven, too.

And what a band of Argonauts—it is Jefferson's phrase—voyaged with him: Franklin and John Adams, Jefferson and Madison, James Wilson and John Marshall, Hamilton and Robert Morris, the two Pinckneys from South Carolina, and Tom Paine whose country was the world, and with these the warriors like Warren of Bunker Hill and George Rogers Clark and Mad Anthony Wayne and Morgan of Cowpens and Nathanael Greene, and the glittering Lafayette who was an American, too: was ever a nation more fortunate in its Founding Fathers? And as if to demonstrate providential approval, the generation that fought the Revolution and won independence survived to create the new nation, expand it to the Mississippi and beyond, and direct its destinies for half a century.

Jefferson and John Adams who had signed the Declaration of Independence lived on into the administration of John Quincy Adams and both died precisely fifty years after the signing. All the early presidents came out of the Revolution: Washington, Adams, Jefferson, Madison, Monroe; even their successors, John Quincy Adams and Andrew Jackson, had seen something of the Revolution—Adams who had been with his father in Paris when the British acknowledged American independence, Jackson who wore all his life the scar of a saber wound inflicted on him by a British redcoat. The generation of Americans who created American nationalism did not need an Alfred, a Joan of Arc, a Frederick Barbarossa; their legendary heroes were still with them.

Nationalism in the Old World was nourished on symbols which conjured up a common past and provided the common denominators of common allusions and associations. Americans, who had no common past (not by European standards anyway) provided themselves with a usable past with astonishing speed and effectiveness. What a profusion of symbols and associations emerged, almost overnight. The bald eagle did not compare badly with the British lion, and was somewhat more at home in America than the lion in Britain, and Uncle Sam was quite as good as John Bull and certainly more democratic. The Stars and Stripes, if it did not fall straight out of Heaven, like the Danish Dannebrog, quickly achieved its own mythology and boasted, besides, one inestimable advantage over all other flags, in that it provided an adjustable key to geography and a visible testimony to growth. The Declaration of Independence was a good deal easier to understand than Magna Carta, and parts of it could be memorized and recited, as Magna Carta could not; in addition, it had a Liberty Bell to toll its fame. There were, in no time at all, no fewer than three national mottoes: *E Pluribus Unum*, which could be taken not only to mean that the separate states made one nation, but that the different racial and ethnic groups did, too; *Novus Ordo Saeculorum*, a new order of the ages; and the Virgilian *Annuit Coeptis*, which announced—rightly, too—that God favored their enterprise. There were no antiquities, unless Plymouth Rock or Indian mounds could qualify, but there were shrines a-plenty: the Charter Oak and the Cambridge Elm, Independence Hall and Faneuil Hall, Bunker Hill and Valley Forge, and the Constitution itself, which, as Tom Paine wrote, took the place of the king in America, and, in time, there were Mount Vernon and Monticello.

FEDERATION AND AN END TO COLONIALISM

THEY CREATED a nation, then, and provided it, almost overnight, with some of those cultural and emotional associations so essential to national unity. But their real genius was for the practical, and their most significant accomplishments in the realm of political institutions. Thus they solved, with what now seems consummate ease, the two intractable problems of colonialism and of federalism. No other modern nation had known what to do with colonies except to exploit them for the benefit of the mother country, a policy which persisted into the twentieth century.

Even Britain, the most enlightened of eighteenth-century empires, fell back, in a crisis, on the philosophy of the Declaratory Act, that colonies are, and of right ought to be, subordinate in all cases whatsoever to the mother country; even in Britain—as Franklin observed—every Tom, Dick, and Harry hoisted himself on the throne of the king and talked about "our colonies" in America. The new United States was born a great colonial power, with a hinterland larger than the original thirteen states; it was to be, in the course of the nineteenth century, the greatest of colonizing powers. What was to be the policy toward that vast hinterland that stretched westward to the Mississippi and—within the lifetime of men who had lived through the Revolution—to the Pacific? Was the West to be held in a state of pupilage, or exploited for the benefit of the "mother country" along the Atlantic seaboard? Had the Founding Fathers embraced that policy, the United States today might be a dozen countries, not one. Happily wiser counsels prevailed. By the simple device of transforming colonies into states and admitting these to the Union on the basis of absolute equality with the original states—a policy proclaimed in the Congressional Resolution of 1780, suffusing the two great land ordinances of 1784 and 1785 (both written or inspired by Jefferson) and finally enshrined in the great Northwest Ordinance of 1787—Americans substituted the great principle of the co-ordinate state for the malign principle of colonialism.

"Thirteen clocks were made to strike together," John Adams was to write. How did they bring about this miracle? How did they solve the problem of federalism whose solution had eluded every state from the days of the ancient Greek confederations and the federations of medieval Italy down to the Helvetic confederacy and the Dutch confederacy and even the old British empire—an empire federal in functioning, though not in logic or in law? All previous confederations had been either too strong in the center or in the parts. Even the Americans were unable—or unwilling—to decide whether sovereignty inhered in the states or in the nation.

Instead, by what we can now see was a stroke of political genius, they by-passed the question and located sovereignty in the people, who, in turn, distributed between state and nation such powers as were appropriate to each government. The Founding Fathers saw clearly enough that this distribution of powers between national and state governments was fraught with difficulties; they sought to circumvent these by providing that the Constitution, and the laws in pursuance thereof, should always be the *supreme* law of the land and that the judges of the states should be bound thereby. This worked well enough in most ordinary controversies; it did not work to settle the problem of states' rights in the arena of slavery; but then nothing would have worked in that tortured arena. Once slavery was out of the way, the national authority was restored much as Madison had originally planned; thereafter, the problem of the division of authority between state and nation was troublesome, but no longer threatened the integrity of the nation.

THE SOVEREIGN PEOPLE

ALL VERY WELL to say that the Founding Fathers made a nation. But so, it might be said, Peter the Great made the Russian nation, or Frederick II made Prussia, Napoleon made modern France, Bolívar made Colombia, and Iturbide, Mexico. But the American process was fundamentally different from all of these, and the analogies wholly irrelevant. For who, after all, were the Founding Fathers—who but the elected representatives of the American people. In the states, and on the national scene, it was the American people who were the makers, not a handful of rulers or chieftains.

Representative government and the common law were brought to these shores by the Jamestown settlers, who arrived in 1607. The first legislative assembly in the New World met at Jamestown in 1619. The English common law was brought to this country in the previous year by those same settlers in their "Greate Charter," and was taken for granted everywhere in the colonies.

From the landfall at Plymouth thoughtful Americans had accepted the principle that government is made by "compact" (the Puritans preferred the term "covenant"), and over the years they came to take pretty much for granted that governments so made "derive" all their powers from the consent of the governed. Certainly Thomas Jefferson did not originate this theory. It had been tried out briefly in Commonwealth England and then rejected by Cromwell himself and later and more decisively, by Charles II; it had been reformulated by John Locke in his *Two Treatises on Government* and given a more romantic gloss by Rousseau. But nowhere in eighteenth-century Europe was it taken seriously by those who designed the political fabric.

It is fascinating to see how even during the crisis and turmoil of war, Americans did take this principle seriously—how they took for granted that the source of all authority was in the people, and that the people had an indubitable right to alter or abolish governments and institute new. Yet this was not really surprising. Nature—or history—is always aping art, and the methods of making a government, which Locke and Rousseau imagined to belong to some fabulous age and which modern sociologists insist belong only to the mythology, had been familiar to Americans since the Mayflower Compact, and the Fundamental Orders of Connecticut of 1639. What was farfetched theory in the Old World was the common sense of the matter—nay the necessity of the matter—in one American community after another. Here is stout John Adams explaining to the Continental Congress the elementary principles of state-making:

> I had looked into the ancient and modern confederacies for examples, but they all appeared to me to have been huddled up in a hurry by a few chiefs. But we had a people of more intelligence, curiosity and enterprise, *who must all be consulted*, and we must realize the theories of the wisest writers, and invite the people to erect the whole building with their own hands upon the broadest foundations . . . for the people were the source of all authority and the original of all power.

Here is a group of "Mechanicks" of New York City, informing their representatives that

> to judge whether it be consistent with their interest to accept or reject a Constitution framed for that State of which they are members . . . is the birthright of every man to whatever state he may belong. There he is, or ought to be, by inalienable right, a co-legislator with all the other members of that community.

Here is a town meeting in the frontier town of Hanover in New Hampshire asserting that "all power originates from the people. A state of independency before a plan of government is formed supposes the whole right to be vested in them who by a full representation are to rear a new fabric." Best of all, listen to Richard Henderson addressing the representatives of four little settlements in frontier Kentucky in 1775:

> If any doubt remain amongst you with respect to the force or efficacy of whatever laws you now or hereafter make, be pleased to consider that all power is originally

in the people; therefore, make it their interest by impartial and beneficial laws, and you may be sure of their inclination to see them enforced. For it is not to be supposed that a people, anxious and desirous of having laws made, who approve of the method of choosing representatives to meet in General Convention for that purpose can want the necessary and concomitant virtue to carry them into execution.

And he reminded them, with that eloquence which seemed so natural to the generation of the Founding Fathers, that

you are fixing the palladium, or placing the first cornerstone of an edifice, the height and magnificence of whose superstructure is now in the womb of futurity, and can only become great and glorious in proportion to the excellence of its foundation.

DEMOCRACY'S FUNDAMENTAL INSTRUMENT

N O W O N D E R the institutionalization of the basic principle that men make government seemed so easy. It was achieved through the constitutional convention, a contrivance which has some claim to be the most important political instrument of democracy, for it provides the essential mechanism whereby men can come together in their sovereign capacity to create governments. More, it provides a legal method for men to "alter or abolish" governments—to alter by amendment, to abolish by wiping the slate clean and drawing up a new constitution. Thus, for the first time in history, men legalized revolution. As Alexander Hamilton wrote, the Constitutional Convention "substituted the mild magistracy of the law for the violent and sanguinary agency of the sword." Thomas Jefferson put it more elaborately. "Happy for us," he said

that when we find our constitutions defective and insufficient to secure the happiness of our people, we can assemble with all the coolness of philosophers and set it to rights, while every other nation on earth must have recourse to arms to amend or to restore their constitutions.

That is substantially true even today.

Revolutionary America, then, institutionalized the principle that men make government. But *what* men make government? The constitutional convention represented the *principle* of democracy; its practice—that is, its reality—was to be found in such things as suffrage and officeholding. In these areas it is inescapably clear that Americans instituted, during the revolutionary era, the most democratic governments to be found in the western world. They were not wholly democratic by our standards, for suffrage and officeholding were pretty well limited to white adult males and, in some states, to professing Christians and to those with some tangible property. The limitations on sex and color were, of course, strictly enforced—but so they were, for that matter, until well into the twentieth century. Religious and property qualifications were not, for the most part, taken very seriously: thus, while the Pennsylvania Constitution, for example, limited officeholding to those who believed in God, and in a system of rewards and punishments after death, those qualifications did not prevent Benjamin Franklin, who probably believed in neither, from serving as president of the state executive council.

What is indisputable is that the American states and nation were incomparably the most "democratic" to be found in the world of the eighteenth century. Nowhere else, except to a limited extent in Britain, Holland, the Swiss cantons, and Iceland, was there any suffrage at all, or any thought of suffrage, or indeed any provision for popular participation in the affairs of government. In Britain, with a population of eight or nine million, some two hundred thousand electors had the technical right to vote, and perhaps half that many did; but it is estimated that three or four thousand men—plus the king—controlled the House of Commons. If we look to France, the Germanys, Italy, Spain, Denmark, we discover that there were no elections in which to vote and for the most part no elected officials. Nor, in these countries, did any but the upper classes have access to offices. In the American states almost anyone who could vote could hold office. Certainly that was true in the national arena: how astonishing it was to Old World observers to discover that as far as the Constitution of the new United States was concerned the president, the Cabinet, the justices of the Supreme Court could all be atheists, illiterates, or paupers!

LIMITING GOVERNMENT

SO MUCH for creating a nation and building it on democratic foundations. No less important than providing political power was providing against the abuse of that power. History, which all the Founding Fathers knew so well, taught one inescapable lesson, that everywhere and at all times, government had been greedy for power, that almost all had at one time or another usurped or aggrandized power; and that eternal vigilance was indeed the price of liberty. When Thomas Jefferson wrote that "to preserve rights" was why government was instituted among men, he spoke for a whole generation.

But how place limits on the power of government? No government in the Old World was in fact limited—not that of Louis XIV or his successors, not that of Frederick the Great or Catherine of Russia, not even that of George III and his Parliament: those "facts," which Jefferson was prepared to submit to "a candid world," proved that.

This idea, too, that all government is limited by the great laws of nature and nature's God, as well as by the law of reason, the generation of the Founding Fathers transformed into institutions. What a plethora of devices they contrived to fix limits on government! First, they drew up written constitutions which were, in effect, compacts or covenants that bound government rigorously to those powers specifically delegated to it. Second, they provided for a real, not merely a theoretical, separation of powers and for a complex distribution of powers among the three branches of government, one which was guaranteed effectively to check as well as to balance. Along with these somewhat mechanical checks went practical measures like fixed terms of office, frequent elections, and provisions for legislative—that is, popular—control over the purse and the armed forces. Within a few years they added to this arsenal of limitations something new in political practice, judicial review of the constitutionality of legislative and of executive acts. We tend to date the firm establishment of judicial review in 1803 when Chief Justice Marshall exercised it against a piece of congressional legislation, but its origin can be found in the thinking of the seventies, in the powerful argument of Alexander Hamilton in Federalist Paper Number 78, and in numerous decisions in state and in lower federal courts all through the nineties. Soon the practice became an integral part of our constitutional system, equally useful at harmonizing the federal system, fixing the limits of governmental authority under the Constitution, and educating the American people and their elected officials to the nature of American constitutionalism and to the philosophy of limited government.

BILLS OF RIGHTS

T O   M A K E certain that no government would violate the fundamental rights of its people, Americans added to their constitutions—first the state and then the federal—elaborate bills of rights setting forth in detail just what rights were beyond the reach of government. Britain, to be sure, had its Petition of Rights and, in 1689, its Bill of Rights, but the bills of rights of the American states as well as the first eight amendments of the federal Constitution went far beyond anything to be found in British antecedents, and constitute a new chapter in the history of liberty. For where the English bills of rights provided ample procedural guarantees of justice, the Americans added to these a series of substantive rights: thus freedom of religion, of speech and the press, of petition and assembly. Nor was this the only difference. English bills of rights were ordinary parliamentary enactments; the same Parliament that enacted them could, legally, modify or repudiate them, but in America rights were incorporated into the Constitution itself, and could not be qualified or withdrawn by mere legislatures: they were part of the supreme law of the land.

Contemplate the Massachusetts Bill of Rights of 1780, drafted largely by John Adams. First there is a preamble setting forth the philosophical basis of government and of the sanctity of rights:

> The body-politic is formed by a voluntary association of individuals; it is a social compact by which the whole people covenants with each citizen and each citizen with the whole people that all shall be governed by certain laws for the common good.

Then follows a general declaration of rights—that "all men are born free and equal," and have natural and unalienable rights—among them "the right of enjoying and defending their lives and liberties; acquiring, possessing and protecting property; seeking and obtaining their safety and happiness." Article 4 reasserts the principle that "all power residing originally in the people and being derived from them, the several . . . officers of government are at all times accountable to them." Article 7 makes clear once again the right of revolution, that

> government is instituted for the common good, for the protection, safety, prosperity and happiness of the people, and not for the profit, honor or private interest of any one man or class of men; therefore, the people alone have an incontestable, inalienable and indefeasible right to institute government; and to reform, alter, or totally change the same when their protection, safety, prosperity and happiness require it.

All this is preliminary to the provisions for a long list of particular rights. The bills of rights of Pennsylvania, Virginia, North Carolina, were no less philosophical in their approach to the relations of men and government, and even more elaborate in their catalogue of fundamental rights. And because these rights were embedded in constitutions, because they were couched in terms so broad that they could be adapted to the changing exigencies of government and society, and because their ultimate interpretation and protection came to be assigned to independent courts, they made it impossible for government to exercise tyranny over the minds or the bodies of men (if white) for any long period of time.

The Americans of the revolutionary generation not only succeeded in placing curbs on government, they even acquiesced in placing curbs on themselves—something that almost all political philosophers, then and since, regarded as impossible. For the founders feared not only the tyranny of government, but the tyranny of majorities. With conservatives like John Adams and Alexander Hamilton this was almost an obsession: even

Jefferson, who regarded the principle of majority rule as "sacred," nevertheless added that "that rule to be right must be reasonable." Tocqueville picked up—partly from John C. Calhoun, partly from Justice Story—the theme of the tyranny of the majority and wrote it into his magisterial *Democracy in America*, whence, somehow, the concept, and the fear, entered into the American national psychology. What is most interesting, however, is that so far the only true tyranny Americans have known is that of a minority—the tyranny of slaveholders and their followers over four million blacks. It was the majority that put an end to this tyranny—at the cost of a four years' war—and that eventually wrote into the Constitution and even into practice the principle of equality for all races.

THE POLITICAL PARTY EMERGES

F O R A L L their practicality, the new political and constitutional institutions were neither self-starting nor self-functioning. It remained to create what is, in some ways, the central institution of democracy: the political party, voluntary, independent, and ceaselessly active. Since that original invention, it can be said that there are no democracies without political parties, and that non-democracies do not countenance them.

The political party, as we know it, emerged out of the exigencies of the struggle for independence, and the creation of republican and democratic government. There were, of course, antecedents both in the mother country and in some of the American colonies, and there were analogies in past history, ranging from the factions that plagued the ancient Greek city states through the Greens and the Blues of seventh-century Byzantium and the Guelphs and the Ghibellines of medieval Tuscany to the Hats and the Caps of eighteenth-century Sweden, and the many factions, cliques, and gangs that distinguished British politics after Walpole. These were precisely the "factions" whose dire history could always be invoked to frighten and alarm those who sought to encourage popular participation in government. It was in part to warn against these that John Adams wrote his discursive three-volume *Defense of the Constitutions*, and it was the fear of these that inspired the solemn warning of Washington's Farewell Address, against the "baleful effects of the spirit of party." For party, as Washington admonished his countrymen,

> distracts the public councils and enfeebles the public administration . . . agitates
> the community with ill-founded jealousies and false alarms, kindles the animosity
> of one part against another, foments riot and insurrection and opens the door to
> foreign influence and corruption.

All true enough, as history. But in just four more years Jefferson was able to boast, in his first inaugural address, that "we are all Republicans, we are all Federalists." What had happened?

What had happened was the invention of the modern political party, whose function was to make the political and constitutional mechanisms work. That invention can be dated, with some confidence, to the decade of the 1790s; for as early as 1800 the institution of the political party had taken on those characteristics which were to distinguish it sharply from the factions of Old World countries, and which were to remain with it through the vicissitudes of expansion and growth down to our own time.

First among these characteristics, the party took on responsibility for making politics and government work in day-by-day affairs: the selection of candidates, the agitation of issues, the conduct of campaigns, the harmonizing of legislative and executive policies, and the reconciliation of state and federal interests. Second, parties emerged as national, not local or sectional, and this not withstanding the vast territorial disparity and the potential disparity of economic interests in a nation of sixteen states (for Vermont, Kentucky, and Tennessee had joined the Union by 1800) as large as western Europe. Third, just as the parties did not reflect local or sectional interests, so they did not reflect ideological, religious, ethnic, or class differences. There were, from the beginning, differences of policy, but only rarely—perhaps only once (in 1860)—have American parties espoused those differences of political philosophy which tear a society apart. That is what Jefferson meant when he said that "we are all Republicans, we are all Federalists." Fourth, in America—in sharp contrast to Britain—parties were democratic, in membership, and in leadership. They grew from the bottom up, not from the top down. And what this meant was that parties were democratic in an active, not just in a passive, sense: they provided an opportunity for everyman to have some part in the business of government, for everyman to be a legislator, a president, or a political boss.

These characteristics not only reflected but foreshadowed the nature of political parties for the next two centuries. They reflected, too, those pragmatic features of the American character which were to make possible the peaceful evolution of the American political system down to our own day.

AMERICANIZING THE ENLIGHTENMENT

W H A T   W E   H A V E in all this is a manifestation of the special contribution that the new nation made to the Enlightenment and to modern politics. That contribution was not so much in originality of ideas as in originality of the mechanisms which gave life to the ideas. This achievement was particularly notable in the political and constitutional arena, but spread to other areas as well. The most important of these was doubtless religion. Nowhere in the western world of the eighteenth century, not even in the Low Countries, was there true freedom of religion; nowhere was the principle of voluntarism substituted for that of an establishment. Americans, who, in the words of Roger Williams, "had never known the iron yoke of wolfish bishops," were the first to establish not only true religious toleration (there was some of that in various Old World countries), but complete religious equality and complete separation of church and state. This separation was carried through so easily, and was taken for granted so generally, that even now we fail to appreciate its radical character.

Contrast the American experience with the century-long crusade for some modicum of toleration in France—that campaign whose battle cry was Voltaire's desperate *Ecrasez l'infâme;* contrast it with the role of the Inquisition in the Mediterranean countries; contrast it with the immense power of the church in civil and secular affairs—in government, in the ownership and disposition of lands, in education (as late as 1871 only Anglicans could attend Oxford or Cambridge universities), in exercising censorship, in dispensing justice. But in the new American states religious toleration and equality were established almost as a matter of course. In Massachusetts and Connecticut the Congregational church and in four southern states the Anglican still enjoyed some advantages, but these were swept away within another generation. And as for the United States, anyone who had proposed an established church or giving preference to one denomination over others would have been regarded as demented.

Consider the familiar story of the struggle for religious freedom in Virginia. There the Anglican establishment was as powerful as anywhere in the United States. In the spring of 1776, even before the Declaration of Independence, George Mason of Gunston Hall drafted a declaration of rights that was promptly adopted by the Virginia Assembly; Article 16 provided

> that religion, or the duty which we owe to our Creator and the manner of discharging it, can be directed only by reason and conviction, not by force or violence, and therefore all men are equally entitled to the free exercise of religion, according to the dictates of conscience; and that it is the mutual duty of all to practice Christian forebearance, love and charity toward each other.

SEPARATION OF CHURCH AND STATE

T H R E E Y E A R S later the Anglican church was quietly disestablished. Neither Jefferson nor Madison was content with this: they wanted a permanent separation of church and state. Few favored an Anglican establishment, but there was a great deal of sentiment for continuing some form of state aid to religion in general. Patrick Henry attempted to circumvent the Jeffersonian proposal by the stratagem of providing state aid to all denominations. Madison countered this with a famous "Remonstrance" which rallied popular support to the principle of complete separation, and in 1786 Jefferson's Statute of Religious Freedom was triumphantly enacted. Its preamble is worth quoting for it expressed better perhaps than any other document of the time the American passion not only for religious freedom but for freedom of the mind:

> Whereas, Almighty God hath created the mind free; that all attempts to influence it by temporal punishments or burthens, or by civil incapacitations tend only to beget habits of hypocrisy and meanness; . . . that to compel a man to furnish contributions of money for the propagation of opinions which he disbelieves, is sinful and tyrannical; that even the forcing him to support this or that teacher of his own religious persuasion is depriving him of the comfortable liberty of giving his contribution to the particular pastor whose morals he would make his pattern; . . . that our civil rights have no dependence on our religious opinions, anymore than our opinions in physics or geometry; . . . that to suffer the civil magistrate to intrude his powers into the field of opinion and to restrain the profession or propagation of principles on supposition of their ill tendency, is a dangerous fallacy which destroys all religious liberty; . . . that it is time enough for the rightful purposes of civil government for its officers to interfere when principles break out into overt acts against peace and good order; and finally that truth is great and will prevail if left to herself; that she is the proper and sufficient antagonist to error and has nothing to fear from the conflict unless by human interposition disarmed of her natural weapons, free argument and debate; errors ceasing to be dangerous when it is permitted freely to contradict them.

Jefferson himself described the campaign for the separation of church and state in Virginia as "the severest contest in which I have ever been engaged." If that were true it would cast a roseate glow on the American scene. For no one in Virginia lost his life in this struggle, none went to the stake for his faith, there were no pogroms, no crusades, and none was forced to flee, like the Huguenots, to some more hospitable clime. We cannot but wonder what Voltaire would have thought of Jefferson's observation, or any of the scores of philosophes who wore out their lives in a vain struggle to overthrow the infamy.

The principle of separation of church and state carried with it the corollary principle and practice of voluntarism. In the eyes of the Old World, and of large segments of the New, the notion that religion could flourish without support from the state was as preposterous as the notion that the state could flourish without the church or, for that matter, that morality could survive without the intervention of both. But in fact religion flourished in the new nation rather better when supported voluntarily than when supported by the state. Voluntarism proved as effective in religion as in politics; the principle once established in these areas spread to all others—education, philanthropy, labor, and agricultural activities, until it became, in time, the most distinctive feature of American society.

CIVIL AUTHORITY SUPREME OVER MILITARY

ANOTHER PRINCIPLE that emerged from this revolutionary generation has special significance for our own time: the principle of the supremacy of the civil to the military authority. It is embedded in the constitutional provisions that the commander in chief of the armed forces shall always be a civilian, and that the popular branch of government—the Congress—shall have authority to declare war, to vote or withhold money for the conduct of war, and to share in the making of peace.

These elementary constitutional arrangements reflected a deep hostility to the military and a passion for peace which found expression in many less formal attitudes: thus the commitment to the militia rather than to a standing army; thus the nationwide upsurge of indignation against the innocuous Order of the Cincinnati because it was limited to officers and was hereditary; thus the determination to keep the army to a minimum—it numbered less than one thousand officers and men when Washington took office; thus Washington's moving address at Newburgh in 1783, which effectively scotched whatever plan was afoot for a military takeover, and the readiness with which he himself accepted congressional control and, at the close of the war, retired (like Cincinnatus, as everyone said) to his plantation at Mount Vernon.

The same attitude can be traced in a succession of policy decisions in the early years of the Republic: Washington's famous Proclamation of Neutrality of 1793—the first of its kind in history; the Jay Treaty, which ended the threat of war between Britain and America over the Indians and the Northwest posts, and introduced—also for the first time—the device of bilateral commissions to negotiate solutions to outstanding differences; John Adams's dramatic break with his own party in offering the olive branch to France in the crisis of 1798–99; Jefferson's dedication to peace which extended to the partial liquidation of the tiny American navy and which took historic form in the proclamation of an embargo against powers that threatened American interests—a substitution of trade retaliation for war.

Nor should we fail to note how democratic was the American military. In the Old World military office was the special prerogative of the aristocracy: in France of the *ancien régime* every officer had to boast sixteen quarterings of nobility; in Prussia, at the turn of the century, only twenty-nine out of some eleven hundred senior officers were from the middle classes; in the British army the story was the same, and every British officer, even a lowly second lieutenant, outranked any colonial officer, even Colonel Washington. But the Americans recruited their officers, as their men, from every class of society: farmers, blacksmiths, booksellers, innkeepers, it was all one; the same social equality that obtained in town meetings and in legislatures obtained in the army and the navy. This tradition of democracy in the armed forces lingered on through the nineteenth century and even, though less effectively, into the twentieth.

ALL MEN *CREATED* EQUAL

F O R   T H E   M O S T   P A R T the Revolution was astonishingly successful in transforming ancient ideas into modern institutions, and in making those institutions work. But there was one conspicuous exception to that impressive record of success. That was, of course, the failure to apply the "self-evident truth" that "all men are created equal" to blacks as to whites. It is a failure for which Jefferson and his generation cannot be held wholly responsible, for responsibility here is widespread and persistent; so widespread as to embrace a good part of the western world, so persistent as to glare upon us all through the nineteenth and much of the twentieth century.

What did Jefferson and his associates mean by the term "created equal"? There is little doubt that he used the term in its literal sense, for that is the sense in which the Enlightenment accepted and applied it. What Jefferson meant was that in the eyes of Nature (and, doubtless, of God, if you believed in God) every child was born equal—as, of course, it was. All *subsequent* inequalities—those of race, color, sex, class, wealth, talents—derived not from Nature but from society or government or law. Nature, after all, did not decree the inequality of blacks to whites; Nature did not subordinate the female to the male; Nature did not contrive class distinctions or social or political distinctions. It was not even certain (Jefferson debated this with his friends in the American Philosophical Society) that Nature imposed physical or intellectual distinctions: the American Indian, so Jefferson argued in his *Notes on Virginia*, might appear inferior intellectually and physically to his European cousin, but he had, after all, precisely the physical and the intellectual equipment he required for survival in his own world.

This was not just a Jeffersonian conceit, but a principle generally accepted by the Enlightenment, the pervasive principle of which was that men were everywhere and at all times the same. Nor is it an idea limited to the era of the Enlightenment: the greatest

American sociologist, Lester Ward, was to make it the keynote of much of his sociology. In every hundred thousand babies, he argued, there is the same potential talent in all areas; what happens to that talent is decided by society, which condemns some to feebleness and frustration and endows others with materials for success.

Nor should we forget that the generation of the Founding Fathers tried vigorously to put slavery on the road to dissolution, and that it succeeded in doing so in the Northern states, and in the territory north of the Ohio River. No one contributed more to this crusade against slavery than the author of the Declaration of Independence. As early as 1770—he was just twenty-six—in an obscure case that involved the freedom of a third-generation mulatto, Jefferson argued in court that "we are all born free," and that slavery was contrary to Nature. The court dismissed the argument out of hand, but time did not reconcile Jefferson to the paradox of society proclaiming freedom and perpetuating slavery. His draft of the Declaration of Independence sought to identify the rights of Americans with the rights of Negro slaves, but Congress would have nothing of this, and the passage was stricken from the draft. That fall, Jefferson returned to the Virginia Assembly where, two years later, he introduced a bill to end the importation of slaves—a bill which, he recorded with pride, "passed without opposition"; we should not forget that it was President Jefferson who signed the bill which, at the earliest possible moment permitted by the Constitution, permanently outlawed the importation of slaves. Less successful was Jefferson's bill to end slavery in Virginia by the year 1800 and to train and educate all slaves under twenty at public expense. He did not succeed in abolishing slavery in the whole of the West (that proposal was lost by a single vote), but he could claim much of the credit for the provision in the Northwest Ordinance that outlawed slavery north of the Ohio River. In the end he was frustrated and defeated. "I tremble for my country," he wrote, "when I reflect that God is just, and that his justice cannot sleep forever," and he added that "a revolution of the wheel of fortune is among possible events. The Almighty has no attribute which can take sides with us in such a contest."

EQUALITY FOR WHITES

I f   t h e r e was no equality for Negroes, but only slavery or, in the North, discrimination, white men enjoyed a larger degree of equality than was to be found elsewhere on the globe. There was equality before the law—something that could not be taken for granted elsewhere—and substantial equality in the realm of government and politics. If Washington and Jefferson, the Pinckneys and the Rutledges, belonged to the "ruling classes," the same could not be said of Sam Adams, Ethan Allen, Benjamin Franklin, Tom Paine, and Roger

Sherman—men who would have been excluded from public life in almost every European state. There was equality in the churches, and between the churches, too, and though the Congregational church continued to enjoy some social distinction in New England and the Anglican in the South, both were speedily outnumbered by evangelical denominations. There was equality in the scores of private voluntary associations that already distinguished the American social and economic scene, and equality in schools and colleges as well: scholars did not wear gowns nor sit at "high table," nor did rich students enjoy privileges withheld from the poor.

There were, of course, substantial differences in wealth, and in the ways of life that wealth permitted and poverty dictated, but contemporaries were unanimous that the differences in America were slight compared to those which obtained everywhere in the Old World. By European standards there were no rich, and very few poor. A grateful America did not build a Blenheim Palace for George Washington but allowed him to return, a near bankrupt, to his neglected Mount Vernon, and though Jefferson built himself a Palladian mansion atop his little mountain, it was but a modest reflection of the great Palladian villas that bestrewed the Veneto, by the score, each one of which could have swallowed up two or three Monticellos.

Nothing struck the French and British officers in America during the Revolution more than the absence of beggars, and of real poverty, unless it was the pervasive purity of morals. Americans themselves, to be sure, distinguished between the "better sort" and the "lower orders"; merchants, clergy, planters, men of learning and of family, did constitute the upper orders, and workingmen, fishermen, small farmers, and indentured servants, the lower orders, but the lines between them were blurred and were, in any event, easily erased. Except for the distinctions between white and black, there were no classes in the Old World meaning of the term—no classes, that is, which boasted legal privileges that could be transmitted to children and descendants. It was symbolic that the Constitution itself prohibited the granting of titles, and that though in the ensuing years Americans showed themselves lavish of titles—Doctor, Judge, Colonel, Professor—these were given so carelessly and so promiscuously as to be either meaningless or merely humorous.

The French-born American farmer Crèvecoeur celebrated this social equality in the third of his famous *Letters*. American society, he wrote,

> is not composed, as in Europe, of great Lords who possess everything and of a herd of people who have nothing. Here are no aristocratic families, no Courts, no Kings, no Bishops, no Ecclesiastical dominion, no invisible power giving to a few a very visible one, no great manufactures employing thousands, no great refinements of luxury. The rich and the poor are not so far removed from each other as they are in Europe. Lawyer and merchant are the fairest titles our towns

afford; that of farmer is the only appellation of the rural inhabitants of our country. . . . We have no princes for whom we toil, starve and bleed; we are the most perfect society now existing in the world.

POLITICAL MATURITY OF AMERICANS

THESE ACHIEVEMENTS—the creation of a nation, the contrivance of a federal system, the substitution of the co-ordinate state for colonialism, the invention of the constitutional convention and the drafting of state and federal constitutions, the effective separation of governmental powers, the fixing of limits on government through checks and balances, bills of rights, and judicial review, the transformation of factions into parties, establishment of complete religious freedom and the separation of church and state, the subordination of the military to the civil authority, the abolition of censorship and the guarantee of freedom of speech and of the press, the development of manhood suffrage and the leveling of class distinctions, and the creation of the most nearly equalitarian of western societies—went far to justify Jefferson's faith in the political maturity of the American people and Adams's conviction that "we had a people of intelligence, curiosity and enterprise"; for the achievements were in every sense popular, sustained and carried through by the majority of those who made up the body politic.

Americans were indeed a people of political enterprise. They were also a people fortunate in the leadership unmatched elsewhere in the western world, and unmatched in our own history since that day. A frontier people of perhaps half a million adult white males, spread thin over an immense territory, without a single great city, without a national capital, without the traditional agencies of culture—universities, learned societies, academies, libraries, a ruling class, or a learned class—produced in a single long generation the most distinguished group of statesmen anywhere in the western world. What a calendar an American Plutarch might have compiled: Washington, Franklin, John Adams, Thomas Jefferson, John Jay, John Marshall, George Wythe, George Mason, Alexander Hamilton, Robert Morris, Gouverneur Morris, John Dickinson, and Henry Laurens, and with them the foreign-born James Wilson, Thomas Paine, and young Albert Gallatin who adopted America and whose talents were nourished in the new land.

What explains this outpouring of political leadership, this fertility in the production of statesmen—a fertility unmatched since that day? Some of the explanations are quite practical. There was the elementary consideration that though the American population was small, Americans used what they had. Whereas in the Old World political leadership was pretty much the prerogative of the aristocracy with a sprinkling from the *haute bourgeoisie*, in America it was open to almost anyone who was white; thus though the American population was relatively small, the pool from which Americans might draw their leaders was probably larger than in many of the populous nations of Europe. A second explanation is likewise in the realm of the practical. In the Old World young men of talent had almost limitless choices in their careers: the church, the army and the navy, the professions, banking and finance, the arts and the sciences. They could be soldiers of fortune, they could be social butterflies, they could make a career of being Don Giovanni, as Casanova did. In America young men had a choice of farming, or the countinghouse, of the church or the law. Thus such talent as there was had few effective outlets except in some form of public service.

Not only did America offer few opportunities for the display of talent except in the public arena; it offered few temptations to distract talent from preoccupation with public concerns. Except perhaps in land speculation and the slave trade, there was no quick road to wealth and little likelihood of piling up great fortunes. Washington was one of the large landowners of his generation, but he had to borrow five hundred dollars to finance his travel to his inauguration in New York City; Alexander Hamilton was a successful lawyer and secretary of the treasury, but he was constantly in debt and friends had to come to the rescue of his family after his death; Jefferson owned thirteen plantations but died a bankrupt; Robert Morris, the financier of the Revolution, spent some years in debtor's prison; and Justice James Wilson of the Supreme Court was hard put to escape it. There were few material rewards for military glory or for adventure; soldiers who had served their country well went home to penury, while officers were fobbed off with the promise of public lands, and those who hoped to satisfy their vanity by membership in the Society of the Cincinnati were regarded as monsters of depravity. Nor did Society offer any attraction or distraction; indeed there was scarcely any Society in the Old World sense of the term, for that was a function of courts, of capital cities, of a class system. In the Old World young men of talent might become courtiers or adventurers, but it is difficult to imagine a Lord Chesterfield in America to say nothing of a Casanova or a Franz Mesmer. It is illuminating to recall Jefferson's solemn warning that young men who went abroad to study would lose both their health and their morals, or John Adams's outrage at the avuncular gallantries of Benjamin Franklin, and it is suggestive that the two most famous American adventurers, Benjamin Thompson and Aaron Burr, found Europe more congenial to their talents than America.

Such talent as there was in the New World, then, had few effective outlets except in public channels: in law, politics, the church, or perhaps in commercial speculations. But how did it happen that there was so much talent; how did it happen that American society was prepared to welcome and encourage such talent as there was; and how did it happen that the most striking talent not only went into service to the commonwealth rather than to private wealth, but stayed there?

REVOLUTION AND ENLIGHTENMENT

HAPPY COMBINATION OF CIRCUMSTANCES

THE ABUNDANCE of talent can be explained, in part, by a happy combination of circumstances: a relatively classless society encouraged and rewarded talent wherever it was found, in a Benjamin Franklin, a David Rittenhouse, an Alexander Hamilton, or a Tom Paine; a society with higher standards of literacy than obtained elsewhere in the western world brought out such ability as was available; and the combination of the Puritan tradition and the classical inheritance, which was very strong in eighteenth-century America, put a premium on duty, conscience, and public service. These circumstances go far to explain, too, the readiness of most Americans to accept, and to follow, the leadership of such men as Franklin and Washington, Adams and Hamilton—these circumstances and the elimination of the major body of dissenters, the loyalists, by exile or by intimidation and suppression. Even stronger, however, was the impact of necessity and of challenge. Has any generation in modern history been called upon to do more than was required of this revolutionary generation of a million or so adult white men? They had to assert and vindicate independence, set up state and local governments, "conquer" the trans-Allegheny west and provide for its government, defend their far-flung frontiers against Indians and against the British and Spaniards who hovered on the borders, and create those institutions, political and cultural, essential to the new nationalism. Crisis encourages ingenuity and resourcefulness, challenge stimulates character and creativity. The demands were importunate: it is not perhaps surprising that the revolutionary generation responded to them, but it is astonishing that they managed to satisfy them.

In this, too, we have an early expression of what we have come to think of as the genius of America. It was put, with disarming simplicity, in one of Jefferson's letters to his daughter Martha, who was having trouble with her Latin. "I do not like your saying that you are unable to read . . . your Livy, but with the aid of your master," wrote her father. "If you always lean on your master you will never be able to proceed without him." For

> it is a part of the American character to consider nothing as desperate—to surmount every difficulty by resolution and contrivance. In Europe there are shops for every want: its inhabitants therefore have no idea that their wants can be furnished otherwise. Remote from all other aid we are obliged to invent and to execute; to find means within ourselves and not to lean on others.

It was precisely this ability "to invent and to execute" that distinguished the American philosophers most sharply from the philosophes of the Old World: a genius for the practical and the consequential. The explanation is not wholly in the character of the two groups: Voltaire and Diderot were practical enough, and so, too, Beccaria in Milan and Filangieri in Naples, but they were not in command, and there was little they could do to translate their programs into policy. But in America the philosophers *were* in command, and were able to realize the Platonic ideal of philosopher-kings.

Not that they regarded themselves as philosophers, and certainly they did not think of themselves as kings. They were workingmen, almost all of them, with jobs to do. John Adams speculated and wrote incessantly, but he drafted the Constitution of Massachusetts and was a pretty effective president; Jefferson wrote on everything from architecture to law, from religion to literature, from agriculture to morals, from ethnology to music, but he also managed to write the Declaration of Independence, revise the laws of Virginia, draw up the Ordinances of 1784 and 1785, preside over the first effective political party, and serve as president for two terms. He collected an immense library, but he also created the Library of Congress and provided it with a classification system; he drafted plans for sweeping educational reforms that were never carried through, but he built the University of Virginia; he studied Palladian architecture in the Veneto and sat gazing at the Temple in Nîmes "like a lover gazing at his mistress," but he translated Palladio into Monticello and into the most beautiful university buildings in America and Nîmes into the capitol at Richmond. James Wilson was a political philosopher, but he carried ratification of the federal Constitution in the Pennsylvania Convention, provided the first, and still one of the best, expositions of the new Constitution in his famous lectures at the University of Pennsylvania, and was an effective judge on the first Supreme Court. Joel Barlow was an enraptured poet, whose six thousand lines on *The Vision of Columbus* are still universally unread, but he was a first-rate commercial and diplomatic negotiator and a practical politician, too. David Rittenhouse was a scientific genius whose observations on the transit of Venus in 1769 compared favorably with those at the Royal Observatory in Greenwich, but he drew the boundaries of Pennsylvania and managed its finances during the war. We could go on and on; it is perhaps sufficient to say that Benjamin Franklin was the archetype of them all, Franklin who, in the phrase of the day, drew the lightning from the skies and toppled tyrants from their thrones.

THE PURSUIT OF HAPPINESS

N o w h e r e i s this quality of practicality more impressive than in the American response to, or demonstration of, two of the darling ideas of the Enlightenment—the idea of happiness and the idea of progress. It was not to Jefferson alone that "pursuit of happiness" was an unalienable right: the phrase appears in the constitutions of Virginia and of Massachusetts and has subsequently made its way into half of all the state constitutions. Was the phrase merely rhetorical, or did it carry some meaning? Certainly it has never had any clear legal meaning: no one has successfully challenged any state or federal law on the ground that it denied or restricted his "happiness." Just as certainly it was more than rhetoric: John Adams asserted that "the happiness of society is the end of government, and the happiness of the individual is the end of man," and Washington invoked the concept of happiness five times in a single paragraph of his Circular Letter of 1783: neither man was given to mere rhetoric.

What was happiness? In the Old World it was something that the ruling classes alone could expect to enjoy, though romanticism was already beginning to find it in scenes of rural simplicity. It was the pleasure of the mind and of the senses. It was philosophy, and science, music, and art, it was beauty, it was the graces of life, it was sacred and profane love, and more often profane, it was for some the consolations of religion and of faith. But you could not really expect peasants and apprentices and servant girls to appreciate these things; with them happiness was mostly just staying alive.

In America the concept was a homelier one. It was bread and meat on the table, and milk for children, a well-cultivated farm, a well-stocked barn with an ample supply of wood, the men working their land, the girls and women busy at the spinning wheel or preparing ample meals. It was freedom from a church that collected tithes, from a government that swept young men off to the army or the navy, from poverty and ignorance and superstition. It was children who could be allowed to play, or to go to school, instead of being sent off to service at some great house; it was the right to live where you would, to work at what you would, to marry whom you would; it was the virtue of young men and women uncontaminated by the vices of great cities. Happiness was rural, happiness was peace, happiness was freedom (for whites anyway): so obsessed were many Americans with this concept that they insisted that even their Negro slaves were happy.

We are already on the threshold of what was, for a long time, an essential part of the American credo: that happiness was escape from Europe, happiness was America. This was implicit in Jefferson's letter to his friend Maria Cosway in Paris: "They tell me *que vouz allez faire un enfant*. . . . You may make children there, but this is the country to transplant them to. There is no comparison between the sum of happiness there and here." He put it more formally in his first inaugural address:

Kindly separated by nature and a wide ocean from the exterminating havoc of one quarter of the globe, too high-minded to endure the degradations of the others, possessing a chosen country with room enough for our descendants to the thousandth and thousandth generation . . . enlightened by a benign religion inculcating honesty, truth, temperance, gratitude and the love of man; acknowledging and adoring an overruling Providence which by all its dispensations proves that it delights in the happiness of man here and his greater happiness hereafter —with all these blessings, what more is necessary to make us a happy and prosperous people?

Jefferson knew what was necessary—a government that would "leave men free to regulate their own pursuits of industry and improvement," which followed a policy of peace, and which avoided "entangling alliances" with nations of the Old World.

PRESCRIPTION FOR UTOPIA

T H E J E F F E R S O N I A N program, and that of so many of his contemporaries, is a prescription for utopia. But America was unlike the hundreds of utopias imagined by the eighteenth-century philosophers of the Old World. These had common, and familiar, denominators: that they imagine something very different from historical reality, that they were revolts against reality, that they were abstract, unrealistic, and mechanical. But the American utopia was a reality: it was not a revolt against the America of its day, but a projection of it into the future. Old World utopias were set on distant and often imaginary places (there were practical reasons here in the avoidance of censorship)—the moon, the underworld, some fabled continent in the Antarctic, the towering mountains of the Andes, or the primeval forests of the Hurons, Abyssinia or Arabia Felix, or, most popular of all, the romantic South Seas, that from Diderot's *Supplement to Bougainville* to Herman Melville's *Typee* had the capacity to inflame the senses of western men.

But the American utopia was located firmly in the United States. It was Pennsylvania, it was Connecticut, it was Kentucky. It accepted America as it was, spacious, rich, and beautiful; it accepted the American people as they were (always excepting slavery), virtuous, prosperous, and enlightened. Old World utopias were all well-ordered, every contingency anticipated and provided for, all the cities of a definite size and pattern, all labor tightly organized and everyone assigned his proper place, family relations and morals all carefully arranged and supervised, even a state religion. But the American utopia left the people alone to regulate, as Jefferson put it, their own pursuits of industry and improvement. No wonder that where European philosophers produced utopias by the hundred, America produced none except descriptions of what actually was, or of what was bound to be. What this meant was that American visionaries—Ben Franklin, Thomas Jefferson, Joel Barlow, Philip Freneau, Ezra Stiles, Tom Paine—were not in fact very visionary, just as American radicals were not in fact very radical. It was visionary enough just to look to the West; it was radical enough just to contemplate American society.

ISOLATIONISM AND EXPANSIONISM

WHERE IT was a matter of the Old World impact on America, the Founding Fathers were isolationists, but where it was a matter of the American impact on the rest of the world, they were expansionists. There was a dilemma here that was never quite resolved. Jefferson and his colleagues knew that they were embarked upon an experiment whose success would be compromised if Americans were to be embroiled in the affairs of Europe, or if they were to be infected with European vices and crimes. Thus for all his cosmopolitanism Jefferson was prepared to reject Europe. Writing from Paris in 1785 he warned against sending an American boy to study in the Old World:

> He acquires a fondness for European luxury and dissipation, and a contempt for the simplicity of his own country; he is fascinated with the privileges of European aristocrats and sees, with abhorrence, the lovely equality which the poor enjoy with the rich in his own country. He contracts foreign friendships which will never be useful to him. He is led, by the strongest of all human passions, into a spirit for female intrigue destructive of his own and others' happiness.

Nor did he ever depart from these views. He supported Washington's Proclamation of Neutrality; warned against "entangling alliances"; invented the embargo as an instrument for peace; called for "a wall of fire between the Old World and the New"; and, when he was eighty, urged upon President Monroe that doctrine which bears Monroe's name. The note echoes again and again: in Barlow's *Vision of Columbus*, which was a vision of a new heaven and a new earth in the New World; in Tom Paine's letter to Betty Nicholson in 1789, with its touching reference to the "innocence" and the "inestimable virtue" of the American character, which "won the hearts of all nations in her favor"; in Freneau's diatribe against England; in Noah Webster's determination to emancipate Americans from slavery to English pronunciation and spelling; and in the Rev. Edward Wigglesworth's proud prediction of an American population of one and one quarter billion by the year 2000.

SPREADING THE BLESSINGS OF LIBERTY

BUT ALONG with this went, not surprisingly, the conviction that America had an obligation to spread "the blessings of liberty" throughout the globe; this imperialism was, to be sure, moral, not military. "Old Europe will have to lean on our shoulders" wrote Jefferson to John Adams, and added exultantly, "What a colossus shall we be when the southern continent comes up to our mark! What a stand will it secure as a ralliance for the reason and freedom of the globe!" When in France he advised Lafayette on the drafting of the Declaration of Rights, and even after the Revolution degenerated into the Terror and the Napoleonic takeover, he could describe it sympathetically as an example of "infuriated man seeking through blood and slaughter his long-lost liberties." When the French armies invaded Italy he wrote with somewhat premature optimism that "the disease of liberty is catching; those armies will take it in the south, carry it thence to their own country, spread there the infection of revolution and representative government, and raise the people from the prone position of brutes to the correct altitude of man"; and at the close of his life he called the Greek Revolution "a holy cause."

Nor was Jefferson by any means alone in this enthusiasm for the American mission. Joel Barlow advised "the Privileged Orders" to follow the American example and forgo their privileges if they expected to survive. Tom Paine went back to England to foment revolution there, and when his *Rights of Man* was suppressed, fled to France to participate there in the great work of revolution and regeneration. Even John Adams, who distrusted all enthusiasm and disapproved of most revolutions, except the American, said that a study of the "means and measures" of the American Revolution may be of use not only to South America but also to all other countries. "They may teach mankind that revolutions are no trifles; that they ought never to be undertaken rashly; nor without deliberate consideration and sober reflection; nor without a solid, immutable, eternal foundation of justice and humanity; nor without a people possessed of intelligence, fortitude, and integrity."

THE CONCEPT OF PROGRESS

CLOSELY RELATED to the concepts of happiness and of mission was the concept of progress; as America illustrated the first, she demonstrated the latter. Here the distinction between Old World and New World concepts was much the same as that of happiness. In the Old World, progress—as analyzed by a Turgot, as interpreted by a Kant, as realized by a Frederick the Great or a Catherine or a Gustavus of Sweden—was either the advance of science and the arts, or it was the growth of the power of the monarch and of the state. Certainly it had little to do with the well-being of the masses of the people, with improving the standards of living, ameliorating the penal code, extending the realm of popular education or of popular culture. There were exceptions, to be sure—a Beccaria here, a Pestalozzi there—but even the most ardent of the philosophes did not think of progress as something affecting the daily lives of the masses. Thus d'Alembert, in his *Preliminary Discourse* to the *Encyclopædia*, the representative achievement of the European Enlightenment, refers to "progress of the mind," to "philosophy," to "erudition and belles lettres" and so forth; thus, forty years later, Dodson's edition of the *Encyclopædia Britannica* equated civilization with "magnificent buildings, noble statues, paintings expressive of life and passion, and poems." And over in Königsberg, Immanuel Kant wrote magisterially of progress that "if it is to come, it must come from above, not by the movement of things from the bottom to the top, but by the movement from the top to the bottom." And in fact that is the way progress was achieved: by the edicts of a Count Rumford in Bavaria, imposing a new regime on the poor, by the Cabinet orders of a Struensee in Denmark, wiping out anachronisms and decreeing enlightened policies in religion and education and public health; by the determination of a Karl Friedrich of Baden "to make his subjects into free, opulent, and law-abiding citizens, whether they liked it or not"; by the decisions of dictators like Pombal in Portugal and Sonnenfels in Vienna.

But in America progress, like happiness, was a combination of material well-being and of freedom for ordinary people, and in America almost all people (who were not slaves) were ordinary. Franklin was the archetype of the American "prophet of progress" as Condorcet was the archetype of the French—poor Condorcet who wrote that *Outline of the History of Progress* and died, a victim of the Terror, clutching it in his hands. But with Franklin progress was better lighting, paved streets, an efficient stove, peace with the Indians, a good government. It was the Junto library, the American Philosophical Society, the College of Philadelphia, *Poor Richard's Almanac;* it was the Albany Plan of Union and the Declaration of Independence, and the Articles of Confederation, the treaty of alliance with France, the federal Constitution. It was moral, too, but even that was a practical matter: remember the famous score-box with the dozen moral virtues that were to be cultivated day after day?

There was one test of progress on which there was all but universal agreement in the eighteenth century—population. As the historian Abbé Raynal put it, "the point is not to multiply in order to make people happy; it is sufficient to make them happy that they should multiply." And from the point of view of the state, population was the incontrovertible evidence of prosperity, of strength, of order—and therefore of progress. By this test there could be no doubt whatever that the American was incomparably the most progressive of all societies. Thanks to the potato and to improved medical care, population was on the increase in many parts of eighteenth-century Europe, in Ireland, Sweden, Finland, Bohemia, and elsewhere. But other nations barely held their own; France, Spain, Portugal, the Italian states, and a few others, owing to wars, famines, or epidemics, actually diminished in population.

But everywhere Americans were obeying the Biblical injunction to multiply and replenish the earth. Here population doubled not in a century, but in twenty or twenty-five years. Thus Jefferson submitted statistics demonstrating that the population of Virginia, slave as well as free, doubled in twenty-seven years; up in New Hampshire the historian

Belknap recorded that notwithstanding the ravages of the war the population of that frontier state had doubled between 1770 and 1790. And not only did population double every quarter century, but the whole country seemed to be a kind of fountain of youth where men and women lived well beyond the Biblical span of years. Better yet, infant mortality was half what it was in so many Old World countries. All this was the product of abundant resources, of rural life, of a social system where mothers could stay home and nurse their babies; it was the product, so Americans confidently asserted, of good government, of simplicity and frugality, of purity of morals. As Hugh Williamson, a doctor as well as a soldier and an historian, wrote:

> The very consciousness of being free excites a spirit of enterprise and gives a spring to the intellectual faculties. If I could speak of our liberties as we speak of the climate and face of the country; if I could speak of their duration as we speak of things that are permanent in nature; I should venture with confidence to predict that in the scale of science the American states, in a few ages, would not shrink from a comparison with the Grecian republics, or any other people recorded in history.

THE END OF THE AMERICAN ENLIGHTENMENT

IT IS DIFFICULT, perhaps impossible, to fix the chronological limits of the American Revolution. Did it begin with the first landing of dissenters on the shores of Cape Cod, with the claims of independence in the Bay Colony's Declaration of Liberties of 1661, with John Wise's *Vindication* of 1717, with Franklin's proposals at the Albany Congress of 1754, or with the Massachusetts Circular Letter of 1768? Did it begin with the defiance of the Stamp Act and the Intolerable Acts, with the meeting of the first Continental Congress and the creation of the Association, with the shots at Lexington and Concord, or with Virginia's defiance of Lord Dunmore? John Adams saw the Revolution as "a radical change in the principles, opinions, sentiments and affections of the people," and wrote elsewhere that "it was already effected by 1775": all the rest was the translation of old ideas and sentiments into new practices and loyalties. It is not easy to quarrel with Richard Frothingham who began his magisterial history of the *Rise of the Republic of the United States* with the New England Confederacy of 1643.

If it is difficult to know where to begin the story of the Revolution, it is even more difficult to know where to bring it to a close. This can, of course, be said of all the great watersheds of history; for the waters that flow the other slope of the watershed gather force, broaden out, and change character until they are lost in the vast ocean of history: thus the watersheds of the Renaissance, of the Enlightenment, of the French and the Russian revolutions; thus, for the Western Hemisphere, the watershed of the revolutions that swept North and South America at the close of the eighteenth and the early years of the nineteenth centuries.

Clearly we cannot encompass all of this in a brief interpretation of the American Revolution but must confine it to manageable proportions and bring it to a logical close. Happily we are not confined to a single moment or a single dramatic episode. For the American Revolution encompassed within itself a series of diverse revolutions: the military, the political, the social, the institutional, even the cultural, each one with its own pattern, though all the patterns were intertwined. None knew better than the Founding Fathers that military victory was not the whole of the matter, nor political independence and the triumph of union. Was it then the acknowledgment by the Old World that the new United States was here to stay, an acknowledgment that can be dated either from the Peace of Ghent or from Jackson's victory at New Orleans? This is perhaps the most nearly logical conclusion to the Revolution; pretty clearly it ends one era and inaugurates another. But independence, like maturity, was a gradual process, marked by a series of climacterics.

FROM THE MOVERS AND SHAKERS

L E T U S T H E N conclude with a series of testamentary notes from the movers and shakers who made the Revolution and founded the Republic.

Listen first to Washington, the embodiment of both revolution and of nationalism, in his Circular Letter to the States of June 1783, as he celebrated the end of the times that tried men's souls and admonished his countrymen to take their place on that "conspicuous Theatre . . . peculiarly designated by Providence for the display of human greatness and felicity."

> The foundation of our Empire was not laid in the gloomy age of Ignorance and Superstition, but at an Epocha when the rights of mankind were better understood and more clearly defined, than at any former period, the researches of the human mind after social happiness have been carried to a great extent, the Treasures of knowledge, acquired by the labours of Philosophers, Sages and Legislatures . . . laid open for our use, and their collected wisdom may be happily applied in the Establishment of our forms of Government; the free Cultivation of Letters, the unbounded extension of Commerce, the progressive refinement of Manners, the growing liberality of sentiment, and, above all, the pure and benign light of Revelation have had a meliorating influence on Mankind and increased the bless-

ings of Society. At this auspicious period the United States came into existence as a Nation, and if their Citizens should not be completely free and happy, the fault will be entirely their own.

Only four years later—so headlong was the rush of events—the generation that had won the Revolution had put together a union and drafted a new Constitution, and three of its major architects undertook to explain and to vindicate their handiwork. Here is James Madison, who has a better claim than any other to be considered the Father of the Constitution, writing in Number 14 of the Federalist Papers:

Hearken not the voice which petulantly tells you that the form of government recommended for your adoption is a novelty in the political world; that it has never yet had a place in the theories of the wildest projectors; that it rashly attempts what it is impossible to accomplish. . . . Shut your hearts against the poison which [this unhallowed language] conveys; the kindred blood which flows in the veins of American citizens, the mingled blood which they have shed in defense of their sacred rights, consecrate their Union, and excite horror at the idea of their becoming aliens, rivals, enemies. And if novelties are to be shunned, believe me the most alarming of all novelties, the most wild of all projects, the most rash of all attempts, is that of rending us in pieces, in order to preserve our liberties and promote our happiness. But why is the experiment of an extended republic to be rejected merely because it may comprise what is new? Is it not the glory of the people of America that, whilst they have paid a decent regard to the opinions of former times and other nations, they have not suffered a blind veneration for antiquity, for custom, or for names, to overrule the suggestions of their own good sense, the knowledge of their own situation, and the lessons of their own experience. . . . Happily for America, happily we trust for the whole human race, they pursued a new and more noble course. They accomplished a revolution which has no parallel in the annals of human society. They reared the fabrics of governments which have no model on the face of the globe. They formed the design of a great Confederacy which it is incumbent on their successors to improve and to perpetuate.

Independence and union, so arduously won and so miraculously established, had still to be vindicated. There were many men of little faith—men like the Rev. Jonathan Boucher, who observed (correctly enough) that "a great and durable republic is certainly a new thing in the world," and prophesied its speedy dissolution, or even like Turgot, a friend of America, who nevertheless could write his friend Dr. Price that "in the general union of the provinces among themselves, I do not see coalition, a fusion of all the parts, making but one body, one and homogeneous. . . . It is only a copy of the Dutch Republic, but this Republic had not to fear, as the American Republic has, the possible enlargement of some of its provinces." Even some of the Founders themselves had misgivings about the future: thus Gouverneur Morris, who had been a member of the federal Convention, remembered later that

> fond as the framers of our national Constitution were of Republican government, they were not so much blinded by their attachment as not to discern the difficulty . . . of raising a durable edifice of the crumbling materials. History, the parent of political science, had told them that it was almost as vain to expect permanency from a democracy as to construct a palace on the surface of the sea.

Nor were these sombre predictions animated by malice. The outlook for the new nation in 1789 was indeed uncertain. The pull of local attachments and of state sovereignty was strong: even Jefferson referred to Virginia as his "nation." Vast distances and primitive provision for transportation made unity difficult; and the nation was threatened by Britain from the North and the West, by Spain from the South, and everywhere by Indians. It was the threats from without that were the most formidable. With his Proclamation of Neutrality Washington set himself adamantly against embroilments in the wars of the Old World, and his policy took on almost scriptural authority in his Farewell Address. John Adams endorsed the Washington policy when he made the fateful decision to resist the warmongers of his own party and sent commissioners to France to reopen negotiations looking to the end of the Quasi War. Jefferson, always politically and morally, though never culturally, isolationist, successfully resisted pressure for war during the whole of his presidency. Yet in the end war came, a war which did indeed threaten the integrity of the Union and the survival of the nation. In conduct it was the most wretched of wars but, paradoxically, in its outcome the most successful; alone of our wars it left no heritage of unsolved problems and no aftermath of disillusionment but—thanks no doubt to Commodore Perry at Put-in-Bay, to Captain Macdonough on Lake Champlain, to Jackson at New Orleans, and let us not forget, to Admiral Cockburn busily burning Washington—it left instead, a sense of pride, of glory, of self-respect. It brought, too, the respect of the European world.

That was the background of President Monroe's inaugural address, an address which may be taken as the end of the revolutionary era:

> Never did a government commence under auspices so favorable, nor ever was success so complete. If we look to the history of other nations, ancient or modern, we find no example of a growth so rapid, so gigantic, of a people so prosperous and happy. In contemplating what we have still to perform, the heart of every citizen

must expand with joy when he reflects how near our government has approached to perfection; that in respect to it we have no essential improvement to make; that the great object is to preserve it in the essential principles and features which characterize it, and that that is to be done by preserving the virtue and enlightening the minds of the people.

JEFFERSON'S LAST TESTAMENT

WE MIGHT well conclude with this. But something must be conceded to sentiment and to drama, and we may legitimately conclude our interpretation of the Revolution not with the uncritical self-approbation of President Monroe—a self-approbation shared by most of his countrymen—but by what may be considered the last testament of the man who contributed more to the Revolution and to the Enlightenment than anyone else of his time. The shadows are falling over Monticello, and over the aged Jefferson. It is the twenty-fourth of June 1826, and Jefferson, unable to attend the celebration of the great Declaration at Washington is writing to Mayor Weightman of Washington what proved to be his last letter:

I should, with peculiar delight, have met and exchanged congratulations personally with the small band, the remnant of that host of worthies, who joined with us on that day in the bold and doubtful election we were to make for our country, between submission or the sword, and to have enjoyed with them the consolatory fact that our fellow citizens, after half a century of experience and prosperity, continue to approve the choice we made. May it be to the world what I believe it will be . . . the signal of arousing men to burst the chains under which monkish ignorance and superstition had persuaded them to bind themselves, and to assume the blessings and security of self-government. That form which we have substituted, restores the free right to the unbounded exercise of reason and of freedom of opinion. All eyes are opened, or opening, to the rights of man. The general spread of the light of science has already laid open to every view the palpable truth that the mass of mankind has not been born with saddles on their backs, nor a favored few, booted and spurred, ready to ride them legitimately, by the Grace of God. These are grounds of hope for others. For ourselves, let the annual return of this day forever refresh our recollections of these rights and an undiminished devotion to them.

THE DECLARATION OF INDEPENDENCE

IN CONGRESS, JULY 4, 1776

The Unanimous Declaration of the thirteen united States of America.

WHEN in the Course of human events it becomes necessary for one people to dissolve the political bands which have connected them with another, and to assume among the powers of the earth, the separate and equal station to which the Laws of Nature and of Nature's God entitle them, a decent respect to the opinions of mankind requires that they should declare the causes which impel them to the separation.—We hold these truths to be self-evident, that all men are created equal, that they are endowed by their Creator with certain unalienable Rights, that among these are Life, Liberty and the pursuit of Happiness. —That to secure these rights, Governments are instituted among Men, deriving their just powers from the consent of the governed,—That whenever any Form of Government becomes destructive of these ends, it is the Right of the People to alter or to abolish it, and to institute new Government, laying its foundation on such principles and organizing its powers in such form, as to them shall seem most likely to effect their Safety and Happiness. Prudence, indeed, will dictate that Governments long established should not be changed for light and transient causes; and accordingly all experience hath shewn that mankind are more disposed to suffer, while evils are sufferable, than to right themselves by abolishing the forms to which they are accustomed. But when a long train of abuses and usurpations, pursuing invariably the same Object evinces a design to reduce them under absolute Despotism, it is their right, it is their duty, to throw off such Government, and to provide new Guards for their future security.—Such has been the patient sufferance of these Colonies; and such is now the necessity which constrains them to alter their former Systems of Government. The history of the present King of Great Britain is a history of repeated injuries and usurpations, all having in direct object the establishment of an absolute Tyranny over these States. To prove this, let Facts be submitted to a candid world.—He has refused his Assent to Laws, the most wholesome and necessary for the public good.—He has forbidden his Governors to pass Laws of immediate and pressing importance, unless suspended in their operation till his Assent should be obtained; and when so suspended, he has utterly neglected to attend to them.—He has refused to pass other Laws for the accommodation of large districts of people, unless those people would relinquish the right of Representation in the Legislature, a right inestimable to them and formidable to tyrants only.—He has called together legislative bodies at places unusual, uncomfortable, and distant from the depository of their public Records, for the sole purpose of fatiguing them into compliance with his measures.—He has dissolved Representative Houses repeatedly, for opposing with manly firmness his invasions on the rights of the people.—He has refused for a long time, after such dissolutions, to cause others to be elected; whereby the Legislative powers, incapable of Annihilation, have returned to the People at large for their exercise; the State remaining in the mean time exposed to all the dangers of invasion from without, and convulsions within.—He has endeavoured to prevent the population of these States; for that purpose obstructing the Laws for Naturalization of Foreigners; refusing to pass others to encourage their migrations hither, and raising the conditions of new Appropriations of Lands.—He has obstructed the Administration of Justice, by refusing his Assent to Laws for establishing Judiciary powers.—He has made Judges dependent on his Will alone, for the tenure of their offices, and the amount and payment of their salaries.—He has erected a multitude of New Offices, and sent hither swarms of Officers to harass our people, and eat out their substance. He has kept among us, in times of peace, Standing Armies without the Consent of our legislatures.—He has affected to render the Military independent of and superior to the Civil power.—He has combined with others to subject us to a jurisdiction foreign to our constitution, and unacknowledged by our laws; giving his Assent to their Acts of pretended Legislation:—For quartering large bodies of armed troops among us:—For protecting them, by a mock Trial, from punishment for any Murders which they should commit on the Inhabitants of these States:—For cutting off our Trade with all parts of the world:—For imposing Taxes on us without our Consent: —For depriving us in many cases, of the benefits of Trial by Jury:—For transporting us beyond Seas to be tried for pretended offences:—For abolishing the free System of English Laws in a neighbouring Province, establishing therein an Arbitrary government, and enlarging its Boundaries so as to render it at once an example and fit instrument for introducing the same absolute rule into these Colonies:—For taking away our Charters, abolishing our most valuable Laws and altering fundamentally the Forms of our Governments:— For suspending our own Legislatures, and declaring themselves invested with power to legislate for us in all cases whatsoever.—He has abdicated Government here, by declaring us out of his Protection and waging War against us.—He has plundered our seas, ravaged our Coasts, burnt our towns, and destroyed the lives of our people.—He is at this time transporting large Armies of foreign Mercenaries to compleat the works of death, desolation and tyranny, already begun with circumstances of Cruelty & perfidy scarcely paralleled in the most barbarous ages, and totally unworthy the Head of a civilized nation.—He has constrained our fellow Citizens taken Captive on the high Seas to bear Arms against their Country, to become the executioners of their friends and Brethren, or to fall themselves by their Hands.—He has excited domestic insurrections amongst us, and has endeavoured to bring on the inhabitants of our frontiers, the merciless Indian Savages, whose known rule of warfare, is an undistinguished destruction of all ages, sexes and conditions. In every stage of these Oppressions We have Petitioned for Redress in the most humble terms: Our repeated Petitions have been answered only by repeated injury. A Prince, whose character is thus marked by every act which may define a Tyrant, is unfit to be the ruler of a free people. Nor have We been wanting in attentions to our British brethren. We have warned them from time to time of attempts by their legislature to extend an unwarrantable jurisdiction over us. We have reminded them of the circumstances of our emigration and settlement here. We have appealed to their native justice and magnanimity, and we have conjured them by the ties of our common kindred to disavow these usurpations, which would inevitably interrupt our connections and correspondence. They too have been deaf to the voice of justice and of consanguinity. We must, therefore, acquiesce in the necessity, which denounces our Separation, and hold them, as we hold the rest of mankind, Enemies in War, in Peace Friends.—

We, THEREFORE, the Representatives of the UNITED STATES OF AMERICA, in General Congress, Assembled, appealing to the Supreme Judge of the world for the rectitude of our intentions, do, in the Name, and by Authority of the good People of these Colonies, solemnly publish and declare, That these United Colonies are, and of Right ought to be FREE AND INDEPENDENT STATES; that they are Absolved from all Allegiance to the British Crown, and that all political connection between them and the State of Great Britain, is and ought to be totally dissolved; and that as Free and Independent States, they have full Power to levy War, conclude Peace, contract Alliances, establish Commerce, and to do all other Acts and Things which Independent States may of right do.—And for the support of this Declaration, with a firm reliance on the protection of divine Providence, we mutually pledge to each other our Lives, our Fortunes and our sacred Honor.

John Hancock	*Benj. Harrison*	*Lewis Morris*
Button Gwinnett	*Thos. Nelson, Jr.*	*Richd. Stockton*
Lyman Hall	*Francis Lightfoot Lee*	*Jno. Witherspoon*
Geo. Walton	*Carter Braxton*	*Fras. Hopkinson*
Wm. Hooper	*Robt. Morris*	*John Hart*
Joseph Hewes	*Benjamin Rush*	*Abra. Clark*
John Penn	*Benj. Franklin*	*Josiah Bartlett*

Edward Rutledge

Thos. Heyward, Jr.

Thomas Lynch, Jr.

Arthur Middleton

Samuel Chase

Wm. Paca

Thos. Stone

Charles Carroll of Carrollton

George Wythe

Richard Henry Lee

Th. Jefferson

John Morton

Geo. Clymer

Jas. Smith

Geo. Taylor

James Wilson

Geo. Ross

Caesar Rodney

Geo. Read

Tho. M:Kean

Wm. Floyd

Phil. Livingston

Frans. Lewis

Wm. Whipple

Saml. Adams

John Adams

Robt. Treat Paine

Elbridge Gerry

Step. Hopkins

William Ellery

Roger Sherman

Sam. Huntington

Wm. Williams

Oliver Wolcott

Matthew Thornton

NOTES ON CONTRIBUTORS

(LISTED ALPHABETICALLY)

IRVING BRANT was born in Iowa, January 17, 1885, and graduated from the University of Iowa in 1909.

An editorial writer and editor of various newspapers for thirty-five years, including the St. Louis *Star-Times* and Chicago *Sun*, he is today a frequent contributor to anthologies, magazines, and encyclopedias.

Brant is the author of a six-volume biography of President James Madison, completed in 1961. His books include *Storm over the Constitution* (1936), which strongly influenced the effort by President Franklin D. Roosevelt to reform the United States Supreme Court.

Other books by Brant include *Road to Peace and Freedom* (1943), *Friendly Cove*, a historical novel (1963), *The Bill of Rights: Its Origin and Meaning* (1965), a one-volume Madison biography, *The Fourth President* (1969), and *Impeachment: Trials and Errors* (1972).

KINGMAN BREWSTER, JR., seventeenth president of Yale University, was born June 17, 1919, at Longmeadow, Massachusetts. He is a 1941 graduate of Yale and received his bachelor of laws degree from Harvard University in 1948.

He served on the faculty of the Massachusetts Institute of Technology in 1949–50 and Harvard Law School, 1950–60, returning to Yale in 1960. He was provost when named president in 1963.

Brewster is the author of *Antitrust and Amer-* *ican Business Abroad* (1958) and *Cases and Materials on the Law of International Transactions and Relations* (1960).

His government posts include special assistant to the coordinator of Inter-American Affairs in Washington, 1941; assistant counsel in the Office of the United States Special Representative in Europe (Marshall Plan), 1948–49; a member of the President's Commission on Law Enforcement and Administration of Justice, 1965; named by President Lyndon B. Johnson to a twenty-member National Advisory Commission on Selective Service, 1966.

He is a member of the board of directors of the American Council on Education and of National Educational Television and chairman of the National Policy Panel of the United Nations Association of the United States.

WILLIAM F. BUCKLEY, JR., has been editor in chief of the *National Review* since 1955, a syndicated columnist since 1962, and host for the weekly television show "Firing Line" since 1966.

A native of New York City, born November 24, 1925, and a 1950 graduate of Yale, he has been a prolific writer with approximately a dozen books written since his *God and Man at Yale* (1951).

Among Buckley's books are *Up from Liberalism* (1959), *Rumbles Left and Right* (1963), and *United Nations Journal: A Delegate's Odyssey* (1974).

BRUCE CATTON, senior editor of *American Heritage Magazine* since 1959, after five years as its editor, was born October 9, 1899, in Petosky, Michigan.

He attended Oberlin College and worked as a newspaperman in Boston, Cleveland, and Washington before undertaking a series of government jobs in Washington in 1942.

Catton has written seventeen books about the Civil War; he won the Pulitzer Prize and the National Book Award in 1954 for *A Stillness at Appomattox*, first of a three-volume history of the Army of the Potomac.

Among his other books are *The War Lords of Washington* (1948), *Mr. Lincoln's Army* (1951), *Glory Road* (1952), *This Hallowed Ground* (1956), *Grant Moves South*, (1960), *The Coming Fury*, with William Catton (1961), and *Grant Takes Command* (1969).

JOHN COGLEY, born March 16, 1916, in Chicago, was editor of *The Center Magazine*, Santa Barbara, California until 1974.

Educated at Chicago's Loyola University, he founded and edited the national student magazine *Today*, 1946–48, became executive editor of the weekly *Commonweal*, 1950–55, religious news editor of the *New York Times*, 1965–66, and founding editor of *The Center Magazine* in 1967.

From 1956 to 1964 he was on the staff of the Fund for the Republic and directed its project on blacklisting in the entertainment business.

Cogley is author of *Religion in a Secular Age* (1969) and *Catholic America* (1973). He is the editor of the books *Religion in America* (1958) and *Natural Law and Modern Society* (1963).

HENRY STEELE COMMAGER is John W. Simpson Lecturer at Amherst College. He was for twenty years Professor of History at Columbia University and for another twenty at Amherst College; in between he has held the Pitt Professorship of History at Cambridge University, the Harmsworth Chair at Oxford University, and many other professorships at foreign and American institutions. In 1972 he received the Gold Medal for History from the American Academy of Arts and Letters. Among his many books are *The Growth of the American Republic* (2 volumes) with Samuel Eliot Morison, *The American Mind; Freedom, Loyalty and Dissent; The Search for a Usable Past; Majority Rule and Minority Rights;* and *Jefferson, Nationalism and the Enlightenment*. He has edited the standard *Documents of American History* as well as *The Blue and the Gray* (2 volumes) and *The Spirit of Seventy-Six*. He is coeditor with Richard B. Morris of The New American Nation series, of which some thirty volumes have been published.

ALISTAIR COOKE, K.B.E., was born in Manchester, England, November 20, 1908.

He graduated from Jesus College, Cambridge, receiving first class honors in English, 1929, and was a Commonwealth Fund Fellow at Yale, 1932–33, and Harvard, 1933–34.

Cooke served as film critic for the BBC, 1934–37, London correspondent for NBC, 1936–47, and chief U.S. correspondent for the Manchester *Guardian*, 1948–72.

He was host for the "Omnibus" television program, 1952–61, and "Masterpiece Theater," 1970 to the present.

Cooke wrote and narrated "America: A Personal History of the United States," a thirteen-part television series which won five Emmy awards, and, for himself, the Benjamin Franklin Medal of the Royal Society of Arts. His knighthood was awarded for "his outstanding contribution over many years to Anglo-American mutual understanding."

Among his books are *A Generation on Trial* (1950), *One Man's America* (1952), *Talk About America* (1968), and *Alistair Cooke's America* (1973).

E. MERTON COULTER became Regents Professor Emeritus at the University of Georgia in 1958 after having taught there since 1919.

Born near Hickory, North Carolina, July 20, 1890, he received his Ph.D. from the University of Wisconsin in 1917.

Coulter has been visiting professor and lecturer at numerous colleges and is the author of many books, the first published in 1922. Among those since 1950 are *Wormsloe* (1955), *Lost Generation* (1956), *Georgia Waters* (1965), and *Old Petersburg and the Broad River Valley of Georgia* (1965).

VIRGINIUS DABNEY was born in Charlottesville, Virginia, February 8, 1901, and educated at the University of Virginia.

Editor of the Richmond *Times-Dispatch*, 1936–69, he was awarded the Pulitzer Prize for editorial writing in 1948, and the Sigma Delta Chi national editorial award in 1948 and 1952. He served as president of the American Society of Newspaper Editors, 1957–58, and president of the Virginia Historical Society, 1969–72.

Dabney has been a lecturer at Princeton and Cambridge universities, chairman of the Governor's Statewide Conference on Education in 1966, first rector of Virginia Commonwealth University, and is the recipient of the Jackson Davis Award for service to higher education in Virginia and the Raven Award for service to the University of Virginia.

He is the author of *Liberalism in the South* (1932), *Below the Potomac* (1942), *Dry Messiah* (1949), and *Virginia: The New Dominion* (1971).

Dabney has been chairman of the United States Bicentennial Society since 1972.

ARCHIE K. DAVIS was chairman of the board of the Wachovia Bank and Trust Co., N.A., until his retirement in 1974. He had been associated with the bank in Winston-Salem, North Carolina, since his graduation from the University of North Carolina in Chapel Hill in 1932.

Davis, born January 22, 1911, is a former president of the Chamber of Commerce of the United States and the American Bankers Association. He serves on numerous federal and state commissions, education boards, and on the boards of some of the nation's major companies. He was a member of the North Carolina Senate, 1958–62.

He is a lecturer and writer on the Civil War period.

MICHAEL E. DeBAKEY is president and chairman, Department of Surgery, Baylor College of Medicine, and director, Cardiovascular Research and Training Center, The Methodist Hospital, Houston.

Dr. DeBakey was born September 7, 1908, in Lake Charles, Louisiana. He received his undergraduate and medical training at Tulane University.

He has served as chairman of the President's Commission on Heart Disease, Cancer and Stroke, 1964, and is a past president of the International Cardiovascular Society, the American Association for Thoracic Surgery, and the Society for Vascular Surgery, among others.

His lifelong interest in medical publications is evidenced by the more than 900 medical articles, chapters, and books he has written on various aspects of surgery, medicine, health, medical research, and medical education, as well as sociological and philosophical discussions in these fields.

Best known for his pioneering efforts in cardiovascular diseases, he was the first to perform successful excision and graft replacement of arterial aneurysms and obstructive lesions.

RALPH ELLISON is the Albert Schweitzer Professor in the Humanities at New York University.

A native of Oklahoma City where he was born March 1, 1914, Ellison was educated at Tuskegee Institute and has lectured on American Negro culture, on folklore, and on creative writing at various colleges and universities.

Ellison is a trustee of the John F. Kennedy Center for the Performing Arts and Colonial Williamsburg Foundation.

His *Invisible Man* received the National Book Award in 1953.

JAMES THOMAS FLEXNER, born January 13, 1908, in New York City, is a 1929 graduate of Harvard and the author of numerous books on the American past. His work has been translated into more than twenty languages.

His books on American painting are credited with having helped to inspire the current revival of interest in that subject. *That Wilder Image*, the final volume of his three-volume history, received the Parkman Prize.

Flexner's four-volume biography of George Washington was honored with a National Book Award in Biography and a rarely-given Special Pulitzer Prize Citation. Since then he has brought out a single-volume life, *Washington, the Indispensable Man*. Currently he is publishing a new edition of *The Traitor and the Spy: Benedict Arnold and John André.*

Flexner, who lives in New York City, is also a lecturer.

S H E L B Y   F O O T E is a novelist and historian who now makes his home in Memphis.

A native of Greenville, Mississippi, Foote was born November 17, 1916. He attended the University of North Carolina and served in the armed forces before turning to writing in the late 1940s.

Foote has published five novels, including *Tournament* (1949), *Follow Me Down* (1950), *Love in a Dry Season* (1951), *Shiloh* (1952), and *Jordan County* (1954).

He also wrote the three-volume *The Civil War, a Narrative* (1958–74).

Foote received Guggenheim Fellowships in 1958, 1959, and 1960 and was the recipient of a Ford Foundation grant in 1963. He has also been playwright in residence, Arena Stage, Washington, D.C., and novelist in residence, University of Virginia, 1963.

W .   E D W I N   H E M P H I L L , a native of Wake County, North Carolina, where he was born June 28, 1912, has spent the past thirty years engaged in historical research and publication activities.

After receiving his Ph.D. from the University of Virginia in 1937, he taught history at several colleges. From 1946 to 1950 he was director of the Virginia World War II history program. While director of the history division of the the Virginia State Library (1950–59) he was the founding editor of *Virginia Cavalcade*, a pioneering, pictorial, and popular magazine devoted to the Old Dominion's history.

Since 1959, Hemphill has served in the South Carolina Department of Archives and History and has devoted his efforts mostly to editing *The Papers of John C. Calhoun*, a distinguished series of authentic documents that has now reached eight volumes.

H E R B E R T   A .   J O H N S O N was educated at Columbia University, receiving his Ph.D. there in 1965. He received his law degree from the New York Law School and was admitted to the New York bar in 1960.

A specialist in early American legal history,

Johnson joined the staff of the Papers of John Marshall in Williamsburg, Virginia, in 1967 and became editor of the multivolume editorial project in 1971.

The first volume of the *Papers of John Marshall* was published in 1974. The project is sponsored by the College of William and Mary and the Institute of Early American History and Culture.

Johnson served as president of the American Society for Legal History in 1974 and 1975. He was awarded the Schiff Fellowship of Columbia University for 1963–64 and a fellowship from the American Council of Learned Societies, 1974–75. His books include *The Law Merchant and Negotiable Instruments in Colonial New York, 1664–1730* (1963), and *John Jay, 1745–1829* (1970).

J E N K I N   L L O Y D   J O N E S is editor and publisher of the Tulsa *Tribune* and a syndicated columnist.

Born in Madison, Wisconsin, in 1911, Jones graduated in 1933 from the University of Wisconsin. Among his numerous awards are distinguished service awards from that university, the University of Oklahoma, and Oklahoma State University. He is also the recipient of the Freedom Leadership Award of the Freedoms Foundation, the American Legion Fourth Estate Award, and the William Allen White Award.

Jones is a former president of the American Society of Newspaper Editors and the Chamber of Commerce of the United States.

H U G H   T .   L E F L E R has been a member of the history department at the University of North Carolina in Chapel Hill since 1935 and a Kenan Professor since 1955.

Born in Cooleemee, North Carolina, in 1901, he received his Ph.D. from the University of Pennsylvania in 1931.

Lefler has written or coauthored many important publications. Among them are *North Carolina History Told by Contemporaries* (1934), *North Carolina: The History of a Southern State* (1954), *History of North Carolina*, in two volumes (1956), and *A History of the United States to 1865* (1960). He edited *John Lawson, a New Voyage to Carolina* (1967), and *Colonial North Carolina: A History* (1973). He has also written articles in many historical publications.

Lefler has served as president of the North Carolina Historical Society, the State Literary and Historical Association, and the Southern Historical Association. He has also been one of the editors of the *North Carolina Historical Review* and the *Journal of Southern History*.

HENRY CABOT LODGE, the president's special envoy to the Vatican, was born July 5, 1902, in Nahant, Massachusetts.

A 1924 graduate of Harvard, Lodge entered politics to serve two terms in the Massachusetts legislature, 1933–36. He was elected to the United States Senate in 1936, and after winning reelection in 1942 he resigned to enter the armed forces during World War II. He was elected to the Senate again in 1946, but lost the seat to John F. Kennedy in 1952.

Lodge was influential in persuading Dwight D. Eisenhower to seek the presidency in 1952 and served as his campaign manager. He was the Republican vice-presidential candidate in 1960.

In 1953 Lodge was appointed United States representative to the United Nations, serving until 1960. He served as ambassador to South Vietnam in 1963–64 and 1965–67, ambassador at large, 1967–68, head of the United States delegation to the Vietnam peace talks in Paris, 1969, and ambassador to Germany, 1968–69.

Lodge is the author of *The Storm Has Many Eyes* (1973).

SAMUEL ELIOT MORISON, author and historian, has been awarded two Pulitzer Prizes.

The first was given in 1942 for his *Admiral of the Ocean Sea;* the second for *John Paul Jones* in 1960.

Morison, born in Boston, July 9, 1887, received his Ph.D. at Harvard and was a lecturer and professor of history there until 1955.

Among his other better-known works are *Oxford History of the United States* (1927), *History, U.S. Naval Operations, World War II,* in 15 volumes (1947–62), *Strategy and Compromise* (1958), *The Two-Ocean War* (1963), *The Oxford History of the American People* (1965), *The Life of Commodore Matthew C. Perry* (1967), *The European Discovery of America, The Northern Voyages* (1971), *Samuel de Champlain, Father of New France*

(1972), and *The European Discovery of America, The Southern Voyages* (1974).

RICHARD B. MORRIS, president-elect of the American Historical Association and Gouverneur Morris Professor of History at Columbia University, was born July 24, 1904, in New York City. He was educated at City College of New York and Columbia.

He has taught and lectured extensively at American and foreign universities, including the Salzburg Seminar in American Studies, and was a member of the American Bicentennial Commission, 1967–69.

Morris is the author of numerous books on the American revolutionary period. Among his books are *The Peacemakers: The Great Powers and American Independence*, which won the Bancroft Award in 1966, *Seven Who Shaped Our Destiny* (1973), *The Life History of the United States* (1963), and *Great Presidential Decisions* (1960).

He has also written extensively on labor and legal history, has edited two encyclopedias, *Encyclopedia of American History* (1953, and bicentennial edition, 1975), and, with Henry Steele Commager, is coeditor of the multivolume New American Nation series, begun in 1953.

MERRILL D. PETERSON, born in Manhattan, Kansas, in 1921, graduated from the University of Kansas in 1943 and received his Ph.D. in history at Harvard University in 1950.

Peterson taught at Brandeis and Princeton universities before going to the University of Virginia in 1963 as Thomas Jefferson Foundation Professor of History.

His first book, *The Jefferson Image in the American Mind*, was awarded the Bancroft Prize in 1961. He is author of *Thomas Jefferson and the New Nation: A Biography* and *James Madison: A Biography in His Own Words*. He is also editor of *The Portable Thomas Jefferson*.

Peterson is a member of the National Historical Publications and Records Commission and serves on the board of directors of the National Committee for the Bicentennial Era.

CHARLES COLEMAN SELLERS, born March 16, 1903, in Overbrook, Pennsylvania, is librarian emeritus of Dickinson College, Carlisle, Pennsylvania, and the author of books and articles on American social and art history, including a succession of studies of the life and work of the Peale family.

His biography, *Charles Willson Peale*, was awarded the Bancroft Prize for 1970.

Other books by Sellers include *Lorenzo Dow* (1928), *Benedict Arnold* (1930), *Portraits and Miniatures by Charles Willson Peale* (1951), *Benjamin Franklin in Portraiture* (1962), and the bicentennial history of Dickinson College (1973).

CLIFFORD K. SHIPTON was director emeritus of the American Antiquarian Society and an authority on colonial America when he died at age seventy-one in 1973.

Dr. Shipton was born in Pittsburgh in 1902 and educated at Harvard University.

In 1930, he became editor of the Sibley series of biographies of all Harvard graduates. He carried the series through the class of 1770. He also indexed the proceedings of the American Antiquarian Society from its foundation in 1791 through 1960.

Dr. Shipton was an instructor in history at Brown University and at Harvard before being appointed custodian of the Harvard University Archives in 1938 and librarian of the American Antiquarian Society in 1939. He became director of the society in 1959 and retired in 1967.

His biographies included *Roger Conant: A Founder of Massachusetts* (1945) and *Isaiah Thomas, Printer, Patriot and Philanthropist, 1749–1831* (1949).

PAGE SMITH, author and educator, was born September 6, 1917, in Baltimore.

He was educated at Dartmouth College and received his Ph.D. from Harvard in 1951. He is emeritus professor of history at Cowell College, University of California at Santa Cruz.

Smith is the author of *James Wilson, Founding Father* (1956), *John Adams* (1962), which won the Kenneth Roberts, Bancroft, and Commonwealth Club awards, *The Historian and History* (1964), *As a City Upon a Hill: The Town in American History* (1966), *Daughters of the Promised Land: Women in American History* (1970), and *The Chicken Book* (with Charles Daniel) (1975).

BRADFORD F. SWAN is theater and arts editor of the Providence *Journal and Evening Bulletin*.

A newspaperman for forty-five years, Swan is secretary of the Rhode Island Historical Society and a past president of that organization.

An authority on seventeenth-century Rhode Island, he has written numerous articles on the colony of that period. He is the historian of the Society of Colonial Wars in Rhode Island and Providence Plantations, a member of the American Antiquarian Society, and a trustee of the Yale University Library.

Swan, a native of New Bedford, Massachusetts, where he was born October 27, 1907, is currently preparing a definitive edition of the letters of Roger Williams.

JOHN J. WATERS, JR., has been an associate professor of history at the University of Rochester, River Campus, since 1969.

The native of New York City, born April 22, 1937, was educated at Manhattan College and received his Ph.D. from Columbia University in 1965. He has held postdoctoral fellowships from Brown and Harvard Universities.

Waters is a member of the Institute of Early American History and Culture.

He has published a number of articles on pre-revolutionary and revolutionary war subjects, and *The Otis Family in Provincial and Revolutionary Massachusetts* (1968), which received the Jamestown Foundation Award.

HAROLD A. WILLIAMS, born April 22, 1916, at Milwaukee, Wisconsin, is the editor of the Baltimore *Sunday Sun*, and the author of seven books.

His books include *Bodine: A Legend in His Time* (1971), *Baltimore Afire* (1954), and *A History of the Western Maryland Railway Co.* (1950).

During his career with the *Sun*, Williams has served as special writer, foreign correspondent, magazine editor, and assistant to the executive editor.

He is a former president and a member of the executive committee of the American Association of Sunday and Feature Editors and a member of the American Society of Newspaper Editors.

THE PATRIOTS

ABIGAIL ADAMS

[1744–1818]

by Samuel Eliot Morison

ABIGAIL ADAMS, wife of the second president of the United States and mother of the sixth, was the most able and articulate of a remarkable group of New England women who were married to prominent leaders of the independence movement in Massachusetts.

Abigail, born November 11, 1744, was the daughter of the Rev. William Smith, Congregational minister of Weymouth, Massachusetts, and Eliza Quincy, daughter of Colonel John Quincy of nearby Braintree. "I never was sent to any school," she wrote in later life; but her grandmother Quincy took her in charge, and she read widely. On October 25, 1764, she married a rising young lawyer of Braintree named John Adams. She bore him five children: John Quincy, Thomas, Charles, Abigail, and Susanna.

During her husband's absence for sessions of the Continental Congress at Philadelphia, Abigail played to perfection the role of patriotic housewife and mother. Her letters give a vivid picture of a country household's privations during the siege of Boston. John loved her dearly and so appreciated her wisdom that he called her his "Portia." When the Declaration of Independence was coming up, she wrote to him playfully, "In the new code of laws which I suppose it will be necessary for you to make, I desire you would remember the ladies and be more generous and favorable to them than your ancestors. . . . That your sex are notoriously tyrannical is a truth so thoroughly established as to admit of no dispute."

During the war, John was absent more often than not; first at Congress and then as one of the mission to France. Abigail carried on through the difficulties of war, blockade, and inflation, and severe New England winters. She joined him at Paris after the peace, in 1783. There followed three years in London, where John was joint minister and plenipotentiary with Thomas Jefferson, and from there she wrote fascinating letters to her nieces describing the court, the theater, and the social life.

Her husband's vice-presidency and presidency (1789–1801) meant, for Abigail, hired houses in New York and Philadelphia and, after 1800, the White House in Washington. The plaster was still wet when they moved in, and Abigail had to use the East Room to dry her laundry with a roaring wood fire. She met the situation with her usual energy and cheerfulness, but was secretly happy that Jefferson's election deprived John of a second term.

The seventeen remaining years of her life she spent at Quincy in company with her husband, in the comfortable mansion he had purchased out of the savings from his salaries. For that he was indebted to the prudent Abigail.

"No man ever prospered in the world without the consent and co-operation of his wife," wrote Abigail truly to her sister in 1809; and she added that, far from being overburdened with cares, she would rather have had too many than too few: "Life stagnates without action." The Adamses celebrated their golden wedding in 1814. John lived to see their son John Quincy become sixth president of the United States, but a sudden attack of typhus fever caused Abigail's death on October 28, 1818. Although secure of a place in history as the beloved and helpful wife of John, Abigail deserves a niche of her own in American literature for the interest and vivacity of her letters.

ABIGAIL ADAMS

by Benjamin Blythe

[MASSACHUSETTS HISTORICAL SOCIETY]

SAMUEL ADAMS

[1722–1803]

by Henry Cabot Lodge

S AM ADAMS speaks to us clearly across two hundred years as the arch-rebel. We do not call him the "father of our country," but he was, in all truth, a prime catalyst of the American Revolution. Indeed, it is hard to imagine the Revolution without him.

It was he who, time and again, said the thing that needed saying, which would never be forgotten—nor forgiven. And it was often what no one else would say. He had the vision of independence when other great figures still hoped for accommodation with Great Britain. He wrote the petition of the Massachusetts legislature to the king protesting the Townshend Acts which taxed articles imported into the colonies from Great Britain. He was the author of the Circular Letter inviting other colonies to help. Some of the utterances in that document so enraged the king that he sent British troops to Boston—and in so doing created a grievance that played Sam Adams's game.

In 1772 he proposed that the towns of Massachusetts appoint "committees of correspondence" to consult with each other about the common welfare—a step which, while not actually illegal, in effect created a revolutionary legislative body that the colonial governor could not reach. At first, eighty Massachusetts towns joined, then other colonies. These committees grew into the Continental Congress. This Congress became the revolutionary government that declared the independence of the United States and administered the affairs of the new nation until 1789 when government under the Constitution began. Sam Adams, with his usual shrewdness and daring, led and managed the virtual state of war which was created when the British sent the tea ships to Boston in 1773. The Parliament in London retorted to the "Tea Party" by closing the port of Boston and annulling the charter of Massachusetts. This helped Adams again by stimulating the first meeting of the Continental Congress.

Finally, the British had had enough. They ordered General Gage, their commander in America, to arrest Adams and John Hancock, whom Gage called Adams's "willing and ready tool." The pair escaped to Philadelphia in time for the second Continental Congress.

This is the barest possible statement of the record of some ten years of revolutionary activity by Samuel Adams. The British Governor Hutchinson called him the "all in all," the "great incendiary leader," the "master of the puppets." General Gage, in offering pardon to one and all, excepted Samuel Adams and John Hancock "whose offenses are of too flagitious a nature to admit of any other consideration than that of condign punishment." Of which Sam Adams said: "Gage has made me respectable by naming me first among those who are to receive no favor from him. I thoroughly despise him and his proclamation."

But Adams was no demagogue. Today he would be described as a "specialist in group violence" or as the "head of the patriot infrastructure." As a manager of men, he was without peer. It is said that he invented the punishment of tarring and feathering and the organizing of groups which today we call "vigilantes." He was always awake, though others might want to sleep, always at work, where others might be tired. He was straight and impetuous, and could be implacable, as he was after the war when he opposed the proposal to restore the rights of the Tories. Could he have lived a second life, the incoming wave of democracy would certainly have lifted him into a place of power. Virginia in 1796 cast fifteen votes in the electoral college for Sam Adams as president.

Perhaps his most characteristic remark came on April 19, 1775, at Concord, which James K. Hosmer describes thus in his biography of Adams:

"In a moment more occurred the incident of Major Pitcairn's order and pistol shot; then while the smoke cleared after the memorable volley, Adams and Hancock were making their way across the fields to Woburn. For Adams, it was an hour of triumph. The British had fired first; the Americans had 'put the enemy in the wrong'; the two sides were committed; conciliation was no longer possible. As the sun rose there came from him one of the few exultant outbursts of his life:

" 'What a glorious morning is this!' "

SAMUEL ADAMS

After Paul Revere

[COPY AFTER AN ENGRAVING IN THE SPENCER COLLECTION, NEW YORK PUBLIC LIBRARY]

BENJAMIN FRANKLIN

[1706–1790]

by *Alistair Cooke*

B ENJAMIN FRANKLIN, the son of an immigrant English dyer and tal-
low chandler, was born in Boston in January 1706, and was brought up in a
turbulent but cheerful household of nine other children. For all his extraordinary
gifts, it may be that the most remarkable was his equable temperament. His
biographers down two centuries have rationalized it variously as inborn wiliness,
a sense of reality, a genius for diplomacy, natural phlegm, and plain common
sense. If he were alive to look into it, he would undoubtedly plow through the
Freudian canon on his way to the prevailing biochemical theories of character.

At any rate, he could face choleric monarchs with unruffled humor, and
court beauties with mischievous familiarity, talk a mob of fifteen hundred frontier
hoodlums out of lynching refugee Indians, and accept the betrayal of colleagues
without petty recrimination. He might well have said what H. L. Mencken said of
himself: "As a child, I was encapsulated in affection and grew fat, sassy and
contented. . . . I doubt that a whole crew of psycho-analysts, working in shifts like
coal miners, would have found anything to go on."

A boy who without any apparent conflict of ambition took as eagerly to the
Latin classics as to flying kites, he grew up with a curiosity unbounded by pre-
conceptions of what was worth knowing and what was not. If political philosophy
was a branch of learning, so was the art of swimming, or the proper management
of the post office. At various times, he devoted himself to refuting the deists,
creating a public library, discovering the positive and negative electrical charges,

inventing bifocal eyeglasses, and expressing his susceptibility to a variety of French ladies in long and elegant love letters.

He was at seventeen already a freethinker, and he went off to Philadelphia, where before long he set up his own printing house, newspaper, and almanac, enterprises that brought him a fortune and left him free to pursue such obsessions as city government, a colonial paper currency, improved street paving, and a firm union of the thirteen colonies within the empire.

On a first visit to England he was received in parliamentary circles as a distinguished statesman and, because of his scientific discoveries, he was cordially admitted to the Royal Society. His second visit, however, coincided with the mounting ineptitude of Lord North's ministry. He negotiated, as a tolerant Whig, for a peaceful settlement of the colonial problem and tried, against heavy sniping at home, to remain a true American and a loyal British subject. But when intermediaries of Lord North offered him a handsome bribe, he became an outright American rebel and went home in disillusion, eventually to take part in the drafting of the Declaration of Independence and to become the elder statesman of the Constitutional Convention.

Even before the irrevocable break, he was sent to France to seek munitions and, in the long run, a French alliance. By skillfully alternating his public image, now as that of an enlightened Francophile, now as that of a plain-spoken, plain-living American republican, he contrived to charm royalists, republicans, and the intelligentsia alike and unite them in their fears of the British. In the end, it was Franklin who brought France in on the colonists' side and guaranteed their military victory.

He died, full of years, friendships, and honors, in April 1790.

BENJAMIN FRANKLIN

by David Martin

NATHANAEL GREENE

[1742–1786]

by Bruce Catton

N ATHANAEL GREENE was the son of a Quaker preacher. In his early thirties, he was a peaceful, industrious ironmaster in Rhode Island, walking with a slight limp and wheezing asthmatically when he spoke, and he seemed an unlikely candidate for military honors. But in the spring of 1775, when the colonies sent military contingents to Boston to join in the fight against British rule, Rhode Island chose Greene to lead its troops, and he emerged presently as brigadier general in the Continental Army.

In the end he became, next to Washington, the army's best general. Twice, in moments of desperate crisis, Washington called on him to save the day. Each time he succeeded.

Greene served in the army's principal battles, became major general in 1776, and played a large part in the famous victory at Trenton, where Washington made his historic crossing of the Delaware.

At Valley Forge, in the terrible winter of 1778, Washington made him quartermaster general, with responsibility for keeping the army supplied. Mismanagement in that important office was at least partly responsible for the legendary hunger that almost destroyed the army; Greene ended the mismanagement, and somehow—by personal drive and the application of sound business judgment and managerial skill—reversed the tide and enabled Washington to bring the army into the spring in shape to go on with the war.

The other great challenge came in the fall of 1780, when the British General Cornwallis all but destroyed the army, inexpertly led by the bumbling Horatio

Gates. After Gates's crushing defeat at Camden it seemed likely the British would establish permanent control over everything south of Virginia—in which case they would eventually get control over everything north of there. Washington sent Greene down to pick up the pieces and halt the drift toward final defeat.

Greene did it. He roundly whipped a British detachment at the Cowpens, crippled Cornwallis's main body at Guilford Courthouse, and then, in a campaign of remarkable skill, kept his own army in being, prevented Cornwallis from coming to grips with him, and by maintaining a Continental force in the Carolinas made it possible for patriot sentiment there to rally and, in the end, won the area for the new nation. Cornwallis, thwarted, marched north to Yorktown and catastrophe, and America had won the war . . . and no small part of the victory was due to Greene.

Interestingly enough, after the war Greene gave up New England and became a southern planter. He died in 1786 on a plantation near Savannah.

NATHANAEL GREENE

by Charles Willson Peale

[INDEPENDENCE NATIONAL HISTORICAL PARK COLLECTION, PHILADELPHIA]

ALEXANDER HAMILTON

[1755–1804]

by Clifford Shipton

H AMILTON was an illegitimate son of an unsuccessful West Indies merchant, a handicap that in that socially conscious age either condemned a man to obscurity or drove him to a brilliant vindication of himself. While an undergraduate at King's College (now Columbia) he wrote political pamphlets so persuasive that they were attributed to some of the great men of his time. He entered the Continental Army as an artillery officer, but General Washington recognized his brilliance and appointed him his aide-de-camp, a position which he made an executive post of great importance. After the war he took up the practice of the law, and by his participation in the Annapolis and Philadelphia conventions did perhaps more than any other man to establish a strong federal union. In the new government he was appointed secretary of the treasury, and by his strong and conservative financial policies, he bound together a union which would otherwise have fallen into thirteen pieces. Virtually the prime minister of the Washington administration, he clashed with Jefferson and the Republicans. Utterly lacking in that diplomacy which alone enables men of different views to cooperate in politics and government, he fought bitterly with President Adams and died needlessly in stubborn pride before the dueling pistol of Vice-President Aaron Burr.

The duel could probably have been avoided, if Hamilton had been willing to answer Burr's questions concerning his criticisms of the Vice-President. Hamilton was opposed to dueling on principle. His feelings were intensified by the fact that his eldest son, Philip, had been killed in a duel a few years before.

When Burr issued the challenge, Hamilton felt that "honor" compelled him to accept. He wrote his wife the night before the fatal encounter that he did not intend to fire on the first volley. There is a conflict of evidence as to whether he did so.

The two men faced each other at 7 A.M., July 11, 1804, at Weehawken, New Jersey, across the Hudson River from New York City. Burr's first shot found its mark in Hamilton's liver and spine. The mortally wounded man was placed in a boat and rowed across the river to the house of William Bayard. In excruciating agony, he died there on the afternoon of the next day, aged forty-seven.

A tragic figure as a politician, Hamilton did as much as any man to create the United States in the form in which it has survived to this day. He had small confidence in democracy, but he was clearly aware that a strong, representative republican union could give the nation a better government than the world had ever seen.

ALEXANDER HAMILTON

by John Trumbull

JOHN HANCOCK

[1737–1793]

by Henry Steele Commager

WHEN THE SECOND Continental Congress convened in Philadelphia in May 1775, it elected Henry Middleton of South Carolina to the presidency. Middleton refused the honor and the Congress turned to John Hancock of Massachusetts, thus quite unwittingly providing him the assurance of immortality. For it was as president of the Congress that, on July 4, 1776, Hancock affixed his signature in large, bold letters to the newly adopted Declaration of Independence. The Declaration was published at once—but not the signatories; it was not until six months later that Hancock wrote to the governors of the thirteen states that "as there is not a more distinguished event in the History of America than the Declaration of Independence, nor any that in all probability will so much excite the attention of future ages." He was forwarding a copy of the document, with the signatures of the signers attached—his own by far the most prominent.

Yet even without the special distinction of that signature, Hancock would have won a modest place in history. Young, handsome, connected with the first families of the colony, and reputed to be the richest merchant in Boston, Hancock had always thirsted for popularity and for fame, and he managed to win both. He had come early under the influence of Samuel Adams who used him skillfully to give respectability to the patriot cause and who, in turn, encouraged him to use his fortune to curry favor with the people of Boston. As early as 1765—he was only twenty-eight—he had protested the Stamp Act; if not the most effective, he was certainly the richest and most respectable of the radicals. Things came to a head when Hancock was charged with smuggling madeira into Boston, and his sloop *Liberty* was seized by the customs officials. Thereafter, Hancock was in the forefront of the opposition to the crown. In 1769, he was elected to the General Court; in 1770, made chairman of the Boston town committee; in 1773, he participated in the publication of the highly damaging Hutchinson letters; and in 1774, he was chosen president of the Massachusetts Provincial Congress and chairman of its Committee of Safety. No wonder the British thought him one of of the most dangerous men in America. One of the objectives of Captain Preston's march on Lexington, that fateful April 19, was to seize Sam Adams and John Hancock.

John Hancock was chosen president of the Continental Congress when Middleton declined the honor; not surprising that he took himself more seriously than others took him. He nursed military as well as political ambitions and was cruelly disappointed when Congress voted to make Washington—not Hancock—commander in chief of the Continental Army.

The next year Hancock withdrew from the Congress and returned to Massachusetts, where he continued his support of the patriot cause and his search for popularity. When in 1780, Massachusetts adopted a new constitution, Hancock was elected the first governor; thereafter he was re-elected whenever he chose to run. When in 1785, he saw storm clouds on the western horizon, he withdrew from the governorship and allowed James Bowdoin to take over. With Shays' Rebellion suppressed, Hancock returned to the governor's chair. In 1788, he presided over the convention called to ratify the new federal Constitution and was happy to be instrumental in working out a compromise between the champions and the opponents of ratification, which brought victory to the Federalists in Massachusetts and encouraged ratification elsewhere in the American states. Hancock was by this time a fixture in the governorship. He died in October 1793, in the course of his ninth term in that office.

JOHN HANCOCK

by Edward Savage

PATRICK HENRY

[1736–1799]

by Virginius Dabney

DESCRIBED BY BOTH Thomas Jefferson and John Randolph of Roanoke as the greatest orator who ever lived, Patrick Henry has often been called "The Tongue of the Revolution."

His fame rests primarily on his oration against the Stamp Act at Williamsburg in 1765—when shouts of "Treason!" were heard from his fellow burgesses—and his impassioned cry for "Liberty or Death" at Richmond in 1775.

Henry's flaming appeal on the latter occasion galvanized the Virginia leaders into action and caused them to authorize the arming and training of military forces for the war that seemed inevitable.

Henry was also a leader in demanding independence at the Virginia Convention of 1776. He served as governor from 1776 to 1779 and from 1784 to 1786. Elected a delegate to the Philadelphia Convention of 1787, called to draft a constitution for the new nation, he refused to go. He feared that a federal charter would largely obliterate the "sovereign states."

When the newly adopted constitution came before the Virginia Convention for approval, Henry led the opposition. His tremendous oratory came close to defeating ratification. He then became a prime mover in securing the adoption of a federal Bill of Rights.

George Washington offered him the posts of chief justice and secretary of state. He declined both.

Such offers from President Washington, coupled with the magnificent phrasing of his immortal orations, should refute the widespread notion that

[75]

Patrick Henry was largely uneducated. In referring to him as a "forest-born Demosthenes," the poet Byron reflected this prevailing misconception. The fact is that he was born May 29, 1736, at Studley, his father's Hanover County plantation, and his father was a judge who had been educated at King's College, Aberdeen, Scotland; his mother came of an excellent Virginia family, the Winstons; and young Patrick could read Virgil and Livy before he was fifteen.

George Mason, author of the Virginia Declaration of Rights on which the federal Bill of Rights is based, said Patrick Henry was "by far the most powerful speaker I ever heard." Thomas Jefferson spoke of his "torrents of sublime eloquence" in the great days of the Revolution.

Henry's health failed in his last years, and he was prematurely old. Washington prevailed on him, despite his enfeebled condition, to become a candidate for the Virginia House of Delegates in 1799. He was the most revered man in the state, with the single exception of Washington himself, and he was elected by a substantial majority. But he never took his seat, for his health declined steadily, and he died at his plantation, Red Hill, on the Staunton River in Charlotte County, Virginia, on June 6, 1799. He is buried in the garden there.

PATRICK HENRY

by Thomas Sully

THOMAS JEFFERSON

[1743–1826]

by *Merrill D. Peterson*

THOMAS JEFFERSON (1743–1826), author of the Declaration of Independence, revolutionary reformer and wartime governor of Virginia, congressman, minister to France, secretary of state, vice-president, then president of the United States, finally father of the University of Virginia, was the premier philosopher-statesman of the new American republic. With humane learning, adventuresome mind, and tireless industry, he raised a house of intellect as lofty and spacious as his Virginia home, Monticello. Architect, scientist, lawyer, educator, agriculturist, musician, bibliophile, philologist, geographer, inventor—Jefferson pursued all these callings, and more, with singular dedication to the building of civilization in America.

The unity of the enterprise was underwritten by Jefferson's faith in freedom and enlightenment. The Baconian axiom, Knowledge is Power, was the core of that faith. Reason and inquiry, he believed, might lead men away from whatever was false, twisted, or capricious in human affairs toward the truth inherent in the nature of things; and thus by the progress of knowledge, vanquishing tyrannical authority and superstition, man might take control of his destiny and secure his rightful estate of freedom and happiness.

A revolution of the mind became the basis of a revolution of government. The work of establishing self-governing political institutions conscripted the energies of the revolutionary generation in America, and Jefferson himself, though he preferred the infinitely more agreeable tasks of the arts and sciences, entered into the service. In 1776 he committed the American government to the inalienable rights of man and laid its foundation in the will of the people. He fought to execute this political design in Virginia; he was a constant friend to "the holy cause of freedom" in a world torn by war and revolution; and in 1800 he presided over the first democratic transfer of power in the nation's history, indeed in the annals of modern politics. Almost any one of his achievements as a statesman—the Declaration of Independence, the Virginia Statute for Religious Freedom, the first plan of government for the American West, the Louisiana Purchase, the Lewis and Clark Expedition, the establishment of a political party that ruled the nation for a quarter of a century—would have been enough to secure his fame were it not secured by his work as an architect or scientist or educator.

But what Jefferson *did* in successive public stations was perhaps less important than what he *said* over a lifetime. For in every avenue of his thought Jefferson enunciated a philosophy of freedom not only for his time but for all time. The voice still rings clear in the oath which encircles the dome of the Jefferson Memorial in the nation's capital: "I have sworn upon the altar of God eternal hostility against every form of tyranny over the mind of man." In the words of Franklin D. Roosevelt upon dedicating the memorial two hundred years after Jefferson's birth, "he led the steps of America into the paths of the permanent integrity of the Republic."

THOMAS JEFFERSON

by John Trumbull

[COLLEGIO DI MARIA S. S. BAMBINA, LODI, ITALY]

JOHN PAUL JONES

[1747–1792]

by Samuel Eliot Morison

JOHN PAUL JONES, naval hero of the War of Independence, was born July 6, 1747 at Arbigland, Scotland, to John Paul, a gardener, and his wife Jean MacDuff, a farmer's daughter. Going to sea at the age of thirteen, he made voyages to Virginia and the West Indies. He rose to be master of ship *Betsy* of London but had to abandon her in 1773 and flee to Virginia because his life was threatened for killing the ringleader of a mutiny. He now added Jones to his name and made many friends, so that when war broke out and the Continental Congress established a navy, he obtained a lieutenant's commission. Promoted captain in August 1776, he received commands of the seventy-foot armed sloop *Providence* and ship *Alfred*, capturing many prizes. Next year he was given command of the sloop of war *Ranger*, then being built at Portsmouth, New Hampshire. On her first war cruise *Ranger* took several prizes in European waters, raided Whitehaven, England, and Saint Mary's Isle, Scotland.

On April 24, 1778, off Belfast Lough, Jones pitted *Ranger* against H.M.S. *Drake*, captured her, and brought her into Brest. Next, he was given command of a mixed Franco-American raiding squadron, his flagship being an old converted East Indiaman which he renamed *Bonhomme Richard* in honor of Benjamin Franklin. Recruiting in France resulted in a total complement of 20 officers (all American except 3 Irishmen), 43 petty officers (all but 16 British), 180 seamen belonging to nine different nations, and 137 Royal French marines. Also under his command were U.S.S. *Alliance* whose captain was the shifty Pierre Landais,

[83]

French frigate *Pallas*, and smaller craft which took no part in the greatest naval battle of the War of Independence.

That took place off Flamborough Head, Yorkshire, on September 23, 1779. A British convoy from the Baltic, escorted by frigate *Serapis* (Captain Pearson) and a sloop of war, ran afoul of Jones's squadron. Hostilities opened at sunset between *Richard* and *Serapis* and continued by moonlight. Mad Landais sailed *Alliance* around the contestants, firing more at Jones than at the enemy. For three hours the two ships grappled board to board, blasting away desperately at point-blank range. At the end of three hours each was a shambles, *Richard* in the worse state, but *Serapis* surrendered before her enemy sank. Jones took possession of the English frigate, patched her up, and sailed her into the Texel on October 3. Thence he departed in command of *Alliance*, and after a prize-taking cruise, put in at Lorient on February 10, 1780.

The spring months Jones spent in Paris, where he met Louis XVI and almost everyone of consequence, and was courted by ladies of fashion. From the king he received a gold-hilted sword and the Order of Military Merit. Returning to the United States early in 1781, he was voted a gold medal by Congress and appointed captain of ship of the line *America*, then building at Portsmouth, New Hampshire. With great difficulty he got her completed and launched in 1782, but Congress presented this fine ship to France.

Now unemployed, Captain Jones managed to attain flag rank, but in the Imperial Russian Navy. Empress Catherine II assigned him to a command in her Black Sea Squadron, then engaged in fighting the Turks. In two battles of the Liman (the Dnieper estuary) Jones and his flotilla distinguished themselves, and the Turkish fleet was largely destroyed. Nevertheless, owing to the jealousy of other foreign officers in the Russian fleet, Jones was divested of his command and dismissed by the empress.

Returning to Paris, he lived frugally on his prize money. President Washington, too late, appointed him American consul to Algiers, with the mission of redeeming American captives. On July 18, 1792, before the word reached him, John Paul Jones died, aged only forty-five. The French assembly gave him a decent burial in the Protestant cemetery outside the walls of Paris. In 1895 his coffin was exhumed, opened, and the body identified and transferred to Annapolis, where it rests in a marble sarcophagus under the U.S. Naval Academy chapel.

John Paul Jones was not only a great fighter and ship handler, unsurpassed in the close combats of the day; he thought deeply on naval strategy, and only wanted command of a fleet in battle to prove himself one of the greatest sea captains of his age.

JOHN PAUL JONES

by Charles Willson Peale

[INDEPENDENCE NATIONAL HISTORICAL PARK COLLECTION, PHILADELPHIA]

JOHN MARSHALL

[1755–1835]

by Herbert A. Johnson

J OHN MARSHALL (1755–1835) fourth chief justice of the United States, was born near Warrenton in Fauquier County, Virginia, and served as an infantry officer in the Culpeper Minutemen Battalion (1775–76) and the Virginia Continental line (1777–79). He was in combat at the Battle of Great Bridge and Brandywine Creek and was wounded in the hand at Germantown. He was at Valley Forge in the bitter winter of 1777–78.

Upon his discharge from military service he studied law briefly at the College of William and Mary (1780) and was admitted to practice in the same year. Rising to prominence in his profession, Marshall was active in the movement for Kentucky statehood and the ratification of the proposed federal Constitution. He served frequently in the Virginia House of Delegates between 1782 and 1798, and also on the Virginia Council of State, and as a judge of the Richmond City Hustings Court. As a member of the Virginia Convention on the ratification of the federal Constitution, Marshall delivered three speeches in support of the Constitution.

The turning point in John Marshall's political career was his appointment as minister to France in conjunction with Charles Cotesworth Pinckney and Elbridge Gerry (1797–98). Although the mission was abruptly terminated by French attempts to extort bribes from the United States in the so-called XYZ Affair, Marshall rose to national prominence by his indignant public rejection of those demands by the French Directory. At the urging of former President George Washington he campaigned for and won election to the House of Representatives, and became one of the few Federalist spokesmen from Virginia in the lower house. Strong in his defense of Federalist foreign policy, Marshall was nevertheless critical of certain domestic programs, including the hated Alien and Sedition Acts. While serving as a member of the House he resigned to accept appointment as secretary of state in President John Adams's Cabinet, assuming a major portion of the administrative burdens of the government. At the end of President Adams's term of office in 1801, Marshall was appointed and confirmed as chief justice of the United States.

Marshall soon began his career as the principal expounder of the federal Constitution. In *Marbury* v. *Madison* (1803) he upheld the principle of federal judicial review of the statutes passed by Congress, and in *Cohens* v. *Virginia* (1821) he affirmed the broad powers of the Supreme Court to review those decisions of state courts that interpreted the federal Constitution, congressional statutes, or international treaties. Within the contract clause of the Constitution Marshall found adequate basis for protecting the vested property interests of landowners and corporations against state legislative discretion (*Fletcher* v. *Peck*, 1810; *Dartmouth College* v. *Woodward*, 1819). He also applied Alexander Hamilton's "loose construction" of the necessary and proper clause, thereby giving broad powers to Congress to effectuate the authority granted to it by the Constitution, and upheld the supremacy of federal legislation over that of the states in monetary and fiscal matters and in certain fields of taxation (*M'Culloch* v. *Maryland*, 1819). Striking down a New York state monopoly of steamboat navigation Marshall established a flexible but comprehensive congressional power for the regulation and encouragement of interstate commerce (*Gibbons* v. *Ogden*, 1824).

Marshall was deeply committed to the revolutionary generation's quest for a union of the American states that would allow a maximum amount of local self-determination within the limits imposed by the national needs for a vigorous economy, a strong national defense, and a unified voice in world diplomacy. It was his sense of history and America's destiny that permitted him to create a balanced federalism that would survive well beyond his death until the United States was shaken by the constitutional revolution of the post–Civil War period.

A tall, ungainly man, Chief Justice Marshall was also careless in matters of dress, leading many to underrate his abilities and to remain unaware of his high station in government. Despite these eccentricities he was extremely popular with his contemporaries, even those who strongly differed with him on political and constitutional matters.

JOHN MARSHALL

by Rembrandt Peale

THOMAS PAINE

[1737–1809]

by Henry Steele Commager

THOMAS PAINE is a symbol of the Age of Reason and the Age of Revolution; he gave the name to the first, and contributed to the second in three countries, America, Britain, and France. He was an American Voltaire; if he had neither the originality nor the profundity of the great French philosophe, he was far more effective in translating his ideas into action. Like Voltaire he had an instinct for the jugular vein of an argument, and a genius for rallying public support to a cause with the telling phrase and the memorable aphorism. As a literary agitator he has never had an equal; by good fortune he was an agitator on what we now think to have been the right side of most issues.

For thirty-seven years Paine had been an obscure and ineffective rebel in his native country of England; in 1774, with the aid of Benjamin Franklin, he came to America, and in the friendly air of the New World his horizons were enlarged, and all of his talents were quickened into life. On January 10, 1776, while Americans everywhere were anxiously debating the pros and cons of independence, Paine published one of the great political tracts of all time, *Common Sense*. It was an eloquent and irresistible argument for independence from the mother country, addressed to the minds and emotions of the ordinary citizen, in a rhetoric at once simple and passionate. It caught the public fancy and spread like a prairie fire; more than any other literary argument it rallied public opinion to the cause of independence. With the war under way, Paine joined Washington's army; late in 1776 he began a new series of papers aptly named *The Crisis*, with the stirring opening line "These are the times that try men's souls." In 1783, he had the happiness to conclude the *Crisis* papers with the triumphant words that "the times that tried men's souls are over and the greatest revolution the world ever knew gloriously and happily accomplished." It was an accomplishment to which Paine had contributed as much as almost any other Founding Father.

Paine was a world figure, but his love for his adopted country was deep and passionate. It was America that had made him, and it was on America that his hopes were centered. "Freedom," he wrote, "had been hunted around the globe; America was the only spot on the world where the principles of political reformation could begin." But, like Franklin and Jefferson, Paine was at the same time a cosmopolite. "My country," he said, "is the world and my religion is to do good." He acted consistently on this principle. No sooner was American independence won than Paine was off to England to raise the standard of liberty. When Edmund Burke denounced the French Revolution, Paine responded with one of the greatest revolutionary tracts in the history of literature, *The Rights of Man.* It was a paean of praise for the Revolution, and a ringing appeal to the people of Britain to follow the examples of America and France by overthrowing the monarchy, ending the class system, and establishing a reign of social justice. Like *Common Sense, The Rights of Man* sold by the hundred thousand and threatened the stability of government in Britain at a time of crisis. No wonder the government suppressed it, jailed the printer, and tried Tom Paine for treason. The verdict was guilty, but Paine had already escaped to France. He was promptly made a French citizen and elected to the National Convention by no less than four departments.

But events swiftly outdistanced Paine; with the fall of the Gironde, he found himself regarded as a reactionary. He was imprisoned by Robespierre, and marked for the guillotine. While in prison he wrote *The Age of Reason*—an assault upon orthodox Christianity—which earned him, quite unjustly, the reputation of an atheist. With the fall of Robespierre, Paine was released from jail. He lingered on in France for another six years, returning to America at the invitation of President Jefferson in 1802. After that everything was anticlimax. Jefferson continued to befriend him, but most Americans had forgotten him, or recalled only his attack upon formal Christianity, rather than his services to the cause of American independence. Alone and neglected, he died in 1809, the most misunderstood and condemned of all the great men who won American independence and made the American nation.

THOMAS PAINE

by John Wesley Jarvis

GEORGE WASHINGTON

[1732–1799]

by James Thomas Flexner

GEORGE WASHINGTON was the indispensable man in the creation of the United States. Had he died before he could play his multiple roles, the entire development of North America would have been very different. The same cannot be said of any other of the Founding Fathers. Had Jefferson or Hamilton or John Adams been prevented from playing his role, history would have been changed in various ways, but the basic structure of the United States would in the end have been the same.

Washington played little part in the agitation that led to the American Revolution, but at the very moment when the Continental Congress took all the thirteen colonies into the war, Washington was officially established not only as the commander in chief but as the public symbol of the fight for freedom. While the Congress, its membership ever shifting, wallowed increasingly in semi-impotence, Washington became more and more completely the power that held the cause together. Military defeats did not endanger his position, since it was clear to all that he could not be replaced. He outlasted four British commanders in chief.

With the approach of victory, there was reason to fear that war would be succeeded by internal chaos. As often happens at the end of a revolution, there was a movement to establish order by the creation of a personal dictatorship. However, there was no one to whom control could conceivably be offered except Washington. His spurning of all temptations for personal aggrandizement set the government solidly on a republican path.

It was by no means certain that when the end of the war made close cooperation no longer necessary, the thirteen colonies would form a single nation. There was the danger that they would coalesce into several groups of states, thus setting the groundwork for such a mélange of nations as would have made the United States into another Europe. Washington's prestige, as was then generally admitted, was the most powerful force that persuaded the states to come together under the Constitution. As the first president, he led in establishing governmental precedents that continued to foster and enforce national union.

Washington was truthfully, as described in "Light Horse Harry" Lee's famous phrase, "First in war, first in peace, first in the hearts of his countrymen."

GEORGE WASHINGTON

by Charles Willson Peale

[WASHINGTON AND LEE UNIVERSITY]

JOHN ADAMS

[1735–1826]

by Page Smith

J OHN ADAMS was pre-eminent among the Founding Fathers in systematic
political theory—his *Defence of the Constitutions of the United States* was the
most comprehensive study of constitutional government written in the era of the
the American Revolution; in his sense of history—after the Boston Tea Party he
wrote "the people should never rise, without doing something to be remembered
. . . This destruction of the Tea . . . is a Epocha in History," and later "the Revolution took place first in the hearts and minds of Americans"; in the vigor and power
of his informal writing; in longevity (he lived to be ninety); and in self-pity. He
was convinced that Franklin and Washington would get the credit for winning
American Independence and Jefferson the credit for establishing the new government on democratic principles while his role would be largely neglected. He was
close to the truth in his gloomy forebodings, but his own contributions were impressive, and today he is finally beginning to get a good portion of the credit he
was so sure he deserved.

From the commencement of the revolutionary crisis in 1765, with the passage of the Stamp Act by Parliament, Adams was a firm if moderate patriot. With
the outbreak of the war he became a strong advocate of independence and worked
assiduously in the Continental Congress to persuade his more cautious colleagues
to declare the states free and independent.

After the alliance with France was concluded, Congress sent Adams to
Paris to join Arthur Lee, Franklin, and later, John Jay, as congressional commissioner. His common sense and toughmindedness contributed substantially to win-

ning a favorable treaty from Great Britain and his negotiations with the Dutch produced much-needed loans to Congress.

Back in the United States after a tour of duty as the first American ambassador to the Court of St. James's, Adams was chosen as Washington's vice-president, and after seven frustrating years in that obscure office succeeded the general as president in 1796. He found, not surprisingly, that Washington was a hard act to follow, and his presidency was beset with feuds and squabbles among the members of his own party and attacks by the adherents of Jefferson.

The close friendship of Adams and Jefferson had already run aground on the rocks of partisan politics when Jefferson defeated Adams in the election of 1800. Adams retired to Braintree disappointed and bitter. After Jefferson's presidency the breach was repaired by a mutual friend, and the two old statesmen carried on a remarkable correspondence during their latter years.

John Adams died, as did Jefferson, on the Fourth of July in 1826, fifty years to the day after the acceptance of the Declaration of Independence by Congress. Not knowing that his Virginia compatriot had died a few hours earlier, Adams's last words were "Jefferson still survives."

No sketch of John Adams would be complete without reference to his wife Abigail, his intellectual and spiritual companion through all his trials and adversities. Their correspondence constitutes one of the richest such exchanges in all history.

To many of his latter-day admirers, John Adams, despite his great achievements as a revolutionary leader, political theorist, diplomat, and statesman, appeals primarily as a superb letter writer and diarist.

JOHN ADAMS

by Charles Willson Peale

[INDEPENDENCE NATIONAL HISTORICAL PARK COLLECTION, PHILADELPHIA]

ETHAN ALLEN

[1738–1789]

by Bruce Catton

E THAN ALLEN was a burly giant of a man who got into the American Revolution because he felt that somebody was trying to do him out of his rights to a parcel of land. Feeling so, he became one of the men who set the struggle for independence on the path toward victory.

Born in Connecticut in 1738, Allen in the late 1750s got extensive land-holdings in what is now Vermont, but which was then known as the New Hampshire Grants. Title came from New Hampshire, but New York also claimed the land, and in 1764 the king of England upheld New York's claim, which meant that the New Hampshire land patents were invalid.

Allen and the other men who held these patents promptly organized a wild, semilawless band known as the Green Mountain Boys, with Allen as colonel, and set out to hold their land by force. When the Revolution began the Green Mountain Boys joined the patriot cause, and on May 10, 1775, Allen led two hundred of his followers to the gates of Fort Ticonderoga on Lake Champlain, where Allen bellowed to the surprised commandant: "Open, in the name of the Great Jehovah and the Continental Congress!" According to another version, he simply demanded: "Come out of there, you old rat!" Whatever the words, the fort was immediately surrendered, England lost a key stronghold in the western country, and captured cannon and cannon balls were hauled east to strengthen Washington's force in the triumphant siege of Boston.

Oddly enough Allen's career thereafter was an anticlimax. He tried to capture Canada, failed and was himself taken prisoner, being held until 1778. His

Green Mountain Boys remained active and had a good deal to do with winning the Battle of Bennington, which helped foil Burgoyne; but Allen's own part was done, and after his release he tried hard to get Vermont recognized as a separate independent republic. This of course never worked, and in the end—in 1791, two years after Allen himself had died—Vermont was admitted to the Union.

He was a hard man to get along with . . . but if any man embodied the very spirit of the demand for independence Ethan Allen was the man.

ETHAN ALLEN

Artist Unknown

[FORT TICONDEROGA MUSEUM COLLECTION]

JOEL BARLOW

[1754–1812]

by Henry Steele Commager

I T W A S an age of paradox and surprise. The age that produced in Benjamin Franklin a runaway apprentice who wrested the lightning from the skies and scepters from the hands of tyrants, in David Rittenhouse a farm boy who re-created the solar system for a stretch of five thousand years, in Alexander Hamilton a West Indian orphan who rose to dictate the American economy, in Benjamin Thompson a warehouse clerk who became prime minister of Bavaria and a count of the Holy Roman Empire, produced in Joel Barlow the most prosaic of epic poets and the most romantic of statesmen.

Barlow came from a little town in rural Connecticut, studied faithfully at Moor's School up in New Hampshire and at Yale College, served as chaplain in the revolutionary army, tried his hand at schoolteaching, editing, business, and the law, and seemed destined for nothing in particular, but he became perhaps the leading American poet (did not Byron refer to him, perhaps ironically, as the American Homer?), a political philosopher, a diplomat, an educator, a Maecenas, and a citizen of the world. Revolutionary France gave him honorary citizenship; he advised the privileged classes of all Europe on the true nature of liberty and equality; he rescued Paine from imprisonment, the *Age of Reason* from confiscation, and American seamen from Algerian galleys; he subsidized Robert Fulton; and wrote two versions of a vast epic poem that justified Columbus's discovery. In his oddly named mansion, Kalorama, on the outskirts of Washington he dabbled with history, poetry, and politics and was part of the inner circle of the Jeffersonian Republicans; appointed minister to France, he pursued Napoleon into the wilds of Poland, and died miserably in Cracow.

It was all very romantic, and the paradox of his life was as ostentatious as the romanticism. Trained to orthodoxy, Barlow ended up rather more skeptical of Christianity than Thomas Paine; steeped in Connecticut conservatism, he had after all collaborated in writing the antirepublican *Anarchiad* and had dedicated the first version of his Columbus epic to Louis XVI. He championed Thomas Jefferson, questioned the sanctity of private property, and celebrated the welfare state. Clearly he belonged not with the Connecticut Wits, but with prophets of progress like Jefferson and Paine, Godwin and Condorcet. Emotionally committed to that New England whose felicities he remembered in *The Hasty Pudding*, he lived most of his adult life in Europe. He was, as he wrote in *Hasty Pudding*

> Doom'd o'er the world thro' devious paths to roam
> Each clime my country, and each house my home,

yet one, too

> Whose heart and palate chaste
> Preserve[d] [his] pure hereditary taste.

A product of the most conventional education, Barlow projected a great research institution which went far beyond anything that Jefferson had imagined for his university, and combined the functions of a Smithsonian Institution, a Library of Congress, and a Columbia University. Passionately committed to the greatness and the uniqueness of America, he envisioned, in *The Columbiad*, an end to traditional nationalism and the triumph of an international order.

All this is not only romantic but improbable; no wonder Barlow is remembered, or forgotten, not for his contributions to politics or diplomacy, but as author of the most formidable epic poem in our literature—3,600 couplets, no less. This would doubtless have pleased him, for it was his poetry that he valued most highly.

JOEL BARLOW

by A. Smith

CHARLES CARROLL

[1737–1832]

by John Cogley

CHARLES CARROLL was born to be the leading Catholic layman of his day; he became a member of the larger American establishment by gambling on freedom. Like most of the Founding Fathers, he was a man of conservative temper; since, in addition, he was very wealthy, the decision to throw in his lot with the revolutionaries could not have been taken lightly.

Carroll's emergence on the national scene began inauspiciously enough in 1773 with his opposition to the imposition of "fees," a euphemism for taxes ordered by the colonial governor against the wishes of the Maryland legislature. The governor's action was thoroughly resented by the colonists.

To sweeten the resentment, Daniel Dulany, a lawyer who was known locally for his skill in handling controversy, came to the governor's defense in the *Maryland Gazette*. Dulany allowed himself to slip into a disastrous *ad hominem* remark. He charged that Carroll was clearly incompetent to discuss political matters because, as everyone knew, he was "disabled from giving a voice in the choice of representatives on account of his principles which are distrusted by these laws. . . . He is not a Protestant."

Inadvertently, Dulany had handed Carroll victory on a platter. Like many controversialists before and since, he had misjudged the mercurial mood of the public. The political and religious climate had so changed that what might have scored a point for Dulany a few years earlier carried the day for Carroll. The anti-governor platform that Carroll supported was upheld overwhelmingly in the next election, and Carroll was credited with the triumph.

After the election, the happy winners flooded the *Gazette* with letters praising Carroll and thanking him for his assistance. Through him, the Catholics of Maryland, probably about one-twelfth of its colonists at the time, achieved their first solid social and even political acceptance. The crude anti-Catholicism that had gone unchallenged for so long became—at least temporarily—passé.

Carroll went on from there. He was elected to various patriotic committees, including the prestigious Committee of Correspondence; later he won a seat in the Maryland legislature. Finally he was sent to the second Continental Congress, where, on his first day in office, he signed the Declaration of Independence, joining twelve Congregationalists, twenty-nine Episcopalians, eight Presbyterians, three Unitarians, a Baptist, a Quaker, and Benjamin Franklin, who styled himself simply as a deist.

Carroll not only supported the Revolution with his private fortune, but put his tested diplomatic skill in the service of the young nation. He was elected to the United States Senate after the war, but later gave up the seat in order to have full time for the Maryland legislature, which he regarded as a more important post.

He lived to be ninety-five, "the last of the Signers"—long enough to see the land of his birth change from a place where men of his religious convictions were deprived of ordinary civil rights to a nation where the practice of any faith or none was protected from governmental interference by a constitutional provision.

CHARLES CARROLL

by Thomas Sully

[STATE HOUSE, ANNAPOLIS, MARYLAND]

GEORGE ROGERS CLARK

[1752–1818]

by Alistair Cooke

GEORGE ROGERS CLARK (1752–1818), commander of the revolutionary forces on the western frontier, is the most wretchedly unsung of all the heroes of the Revolution. Sir George Trevelyan's classic six volumes make no mention of him. Yet, by his military mastery of the long-straggling frontier, he was responsible more than any other man for the British decision to cede all the lands west of the Alleghenies to the United States in the Treaty of Paris.

He left his home in Virginia when he was only nineteen, but when the war broke out he had had five years' experience as a surveyor of frontier lands along the Ohio River. In putting down various Indian uprisings, he had helped to open up Kentucky, but it was doubly threatened in 1776 by the British and their Indian allies. Kentucky had no militia and no authority to protect itself, and it was to secure both that Clark journeyed to Williamsburg and was eventually given the general mission of subduing all the western British forts, frustrating their liaison with the Indians, and converting the allegiance of the French settlements.

This was a commission that might well have appalled any eastern soldier who started to carry it out. Neither Washington nor his field commanders had done much more than engage in sporadic incursions into the new lands. It was the emptiness of the West that impressed them, and they steadily underestimated the problem of conquering it. They tended to plan for numbers and the capture of large settlements. They held to the prejudice that a decisive battle is always a big battle. Clark never succeeded in impressing on them the vast indeterminate extent of the frontier and the nature of a guerrilla war that involved a running

[115]

series of raids and counter-raids, the endless tracking down of Indian scouts, the mopping up of pockets of French resistance.

His first expedition along the Ohio mustered only 175 frontiersmen, but in the early days he succeeded brilliantly, after long marches through insufferable weather, in taking Vincennes and neutralizing British forts to its west. But his attempt to control the north at Detroit was defeated by the reluctance of the eastern command to spare him troops and supplies. He fell back on a smaller fort, Fort Nelson, and from this base, for the rest of the war, he mounted offensives against the Shawnees, and the British trying to secure the West at St. Louis. Most of the time he was devoted to the interminable but essential task of alternately storming small forts, harrying and pacifying the Indians, and breaking up the cement of their British alliance.

He was the most cruelly unrewarded of military heroes. He and his men fought without pay. He was personally debited with the costs of all his supplies, on a promise from Virginia—very belatedly honored—that he would be reimbursed later. To compound this ingratitude, James Wilkinson (who aggravated the mischief between Jefferson and Aaron Burr) forged papers branding Clark as a traitor and alcoholic who had planned a secret expedition in Mississippi against Spain. Clark was accordingly relieved of his last post as an Indian commissioner and was replaced by Wilkinson!

Jefferson later on tried to rescue him from his debts and his disgrace by inviting him to undertake the first crossing of the mid-continent to the Pacific, an adventure he rejected and turned over, as all the world knows, to his younger brother, William, and to Jefferson's secretary, Meriwether Lewis.

He died in penury near Louisville in his sixty-sixth year.

GEORGE ROGERS CLARK

by Matthew Harris Jouett

[THE FILSON CLUB, LOUISVILLE, KENTUCKY]

CHRISTOPHER GADSDEN

[1724–1805]

by Shelby Foote

R EVOLUTIONARY STATESMAN and soldier, self-made businessman and aristocratic leader of South Carolina's propertied, radical "mechanics," Christopher Gadsden was born at Charleston in February 1724. Educated in England, he began work in a Philadelphia countinghouse, served for a time as purser on a British warship, and in his middle twenties, having married, returned to his birthplace, where he prospered so well as a merchant that by 1761, three years short of forty, he owned two stores in town, two in the country, and a plantation. He had served by then the first four of his nearly thirty years in the assembly, and four years later was a leading spokesman for colonial union at the Stamp Act Congress. Impetuous, rash, hot-tempered, he yet commanded the respect of his followers and fellows by his integrity, zeal, and force of character. Willing to submerge his sectional feelings—"There ought to be no New England man, no New Yorker, known on the continent," he declared, "but all of us Americans"— he still felt them strongly all his life, as was shown in a letter he wrote Samuel Adams, midway through the war: "Massachusetts sounded the Trumpet, but to Carolina is it owing that it was attended to; she immediately in 1765 flew to the appointed Rendezvous and had it not been for her I believe you are well convinced no Congress wou'd have then happen'd, and Boston wou'd, if not been entirely ruin'd, continued much longer in her Distresses."

One of the original four delegates to the first Continental Congress in 1774, Gadsden "startled friend and foe alike" at the second, by proposing absolute independence—five months before the actual Declaration. Appointed senior colonel of the South Carolina forces, he was in command of Fort Johnson at the entrance to Charleston Harbor when the British were repulsed in their late-June attack on palmetto-logged Fort Moultrie, across the way, and was made a brigadier in the Continental Army in September. Though a lack of military activity in the Southern Department for the next three years denied him any chance to further his army career, this was the period of his greatest political achievements, including the adoption of the state constitution, in March of 1778, which disestablished the church and provided for the election of senators by popular vote.

On hand for the surrender of Charleston in May 1780, he was at first paroled but then taken to St. Augustine, where, on his refusal to give a second parole, he was put in such close confinement that, as he said later, he "never saw the sun for about eleven months." Released by exchange the following year, he returned to South Carolina and was elected governor in 1782, but declined the office on grounds of age and failing health. Increasingly conservative in the postwar years, Gadsden broke at last with his constituents, though he never lost their respect for his finer qualities. "A man of deep and clear convictions, thoroughly sincere, of an unbending will, and a sturdy, impetuous integrity," the historian George Bancroft was to call him, adding: "He possessed not only that courage which defies danger, but that persistence which neither peril, nor imprisonment, nor the threat of death can shake. Full of religious faith, and at the same time inquisitive and tolerant, methodical, yet lavish of his fortune for public ends, he had in his nature nothing vacillating or low, and knew not how to hesitate or feign."

He lived to the age of eighty-one, and died in August 1805. He was buried close to his parents in Saint Philip's churchyard, in accordance with his will, which also stipulated that his grave was to be unmarked.

CHRISTOPHER GADSDEN

by Rembrandt Peale

NATHAN HALE

[1755–1776]

by Kingman Brewster, Jr.

NATHAN HALE, "Patriot Spy of the Revolution," was born on June 6, 1755, at South Coventry, Connecticut, one of the twelve children of Deacon Richard Hale, a farmer, and his wife, Elizabeth Strong. At the age of fourteen, he entered Yale College, where he established a reputation as a scholar, a fine public speaker, and an athlete. He was the champion wrestler and could kick a football farther than any other student. Both his associates and the college officers testified that he was "unusually attractive and beloved."

Although he had looked forward to the ministerial profession, he decided first to try his hand at teaching. Deeply moved by his country's struggle for freedom from British tyranny, he left the Union Grammar School of New London early in July of 1775 to join the armed forces. Commissioned a first lieutenant, he was assigned to the Third Company in the Seventh Connecticut Regiment, commanded by Colonel Charles Webb.

Things looked bleak for the American cause. General Washington, short of both men and material, was in desperate need of information as to the enemy's strength and plans. For purposes of reconnaissance, a corps of Rangers—130 men and 20 officers—was organized under the command of Lieutenant Colonel Thomas Knowlton. Captain Hale eagerly accepted the opportunity to join this special unit. At a meeting of its officers, Knowlton, reporting that Washington had suggested sending someone behind the enemy's lines to gather intelligence on British preparations and movements, asked for a volunteer. Nathan Hale immediately stepped forward.

He was under no misapprehension of the danger involved in going into New York: if taken up by the enemy, he would, without any question, be hanged as a spy. The risk was amplified by the fact that Nathan's cousin, Samuel Hale (a Harvard graduate), was on duty there as the British army's deputy commissary of prisoners and would surely recognize him if their paths crossed. Nevertheless, the young captain was determined to undertake the mission. A friend and fellow officer, Captain William Hull, who had tried to dissuade him from so perilous a journey, afterward reported that Hale had said:

> I am fully sensible of the consequences of discovery and capture in such a situation. But for a year I have been attached to the army, and have not rendered any material service while receiving a compensation for which I make no return. Yet I am not influenced by the expectation of promotion or pecuniary reward; I wish to be useful, and every kind of service, necessary to the public good, becomes honorable by being necessary. If the exigencies of my country demand a peculiar service, its claims to perform that service are imperious.

Hale traveled to New York by way of Norwalk, Connecticut, and Huntington, Long Island. En route, he changed from his uniform into a plain suit of brown clothes and a round, broad-brimmed hat, assuming the character of a Dutch schoolmaster seeking employment. As evidence of his assumed calling, he carried one important document: his Yale diploma.

Nothing is known of Hale's movements subsequent to his slipping through the enemy's lines except for the final chapter of his life. Apparently caught while returning from his mission, he was searched and found to be carrying notes and plans in his shoe. It was later claimed by his father that Hale had been betrayed by his cousin, but there are no records to substantiate this belief.

Hauled before General William Howe, commanding officer of the occupying forces, the captain made no attempt to conceal his identity or errand. Howe ordered that he be hanged the following morning, September 22, 1776, recording afterward in his order book: "A spy for the Enemy (by his own full confession) apprehended last night, was this day Executed at 11 o'clock in front of the Artillery Park."

Captain John Montresor, aide-de-camp to General Howe, witnessed the hanging and later that day, under a flag of truce, reported to American Captains Alexander Hamilton and William Hull that the spy had demonstrated unusual bravery at the gallows. As the noose was about to be placed around his neck, Nathan Hale said: "I only regret that I have but one life to lose for my country."

NATHAN HALE

Engraved by A. H. Ritchie

[CHICAGO HISTORICAL SOCIETY]

RICHARD HENDERSON

[1735–1785]

by Archie K. Davis

ICHARD HENDERSON (1735–85) was a man of contrasts: a Virginian by birth, he gained fame settling the back country; an antagonist of the Regulators (see below), he soon defied royal decrees in his own business ventures; a firm supporter of the royal governor, William Tryon, in pre-revolutionary years, he became an outspoken patriot during the Revolution; an able jurist, he was at home with such an explorer as Daniel Boone.

Born on April 20, 1735, in Hanover County, Virginia, Richard was about five years old when his parents, Samuel and Elizabeth (Williams) Henderson moved to Edgecombe (after 1746 Granville, now Vance) County, North Carolina. In sparsely settled Granville, Samuel Henderson served as sheriff, and his son Richard became familiar with the most important of the sheriff's duties—the collection of taxes.

With such education as the backcountry could offer, the young man read law and entered practice with his cousin, John Williams. His legal work in court towns such as Hillsborough and Salisbury led to his service from 1768 to 1773 as one of the three justices of the colony's superior court. It was in this position that Henderson first came into prominence, for when the residents of the rural areas—agitated by high taxes and legal fees—organized as the Regulators, they expressed a special antipathy for lawyers and government officials who, they believed, conspired against the farmers. This antipathy led to the burning of Henderson's home and outbuildings in September 1770. Following the militia's defeat of the Regulators at the Battle of Alamance the next May, Henderson with his two colleagues presided over the trial in which twelve of the Regulators were convicted of treason. Six were hanged.

Richard Henderson as early as 1764 had become interested in the transmontane region and had sent young Daniel Boone to investigate the possibility for settlement of the area. Then, in defiance of British policy against white settlement beyond the Indian boundary, Henderson in 1774 organized the Louisa Company, the name of which was changed the next year to the Transylvania Company. In March 1775, he and his colleagues purchased from the Cherokees approximately 20 million acres of land. Boone was hired to cut a road through the Cumberland Gap, and settlers began taking up land in Transylvania, which Henderson proposed to become the fourteenth colony. Virginia, however, refused to recognize the company's claims, and the settlers were soon absorbed into the new Virginia county of Kentucky.

In 1779 Henderson was appointed to head North Carolina's commission to settle its boundary with Virginia in the west. The survey revealed that a portion of the Transylvania Company tract lay in North Carolina's western territory. Henderson thereupon joined James Robertson and others in establishing a settlement at French Lick, the site of the present city of Nashville (originally named Nashborough after General Francis Nash). Henderson's handwritten Cumberland Compact—both a constitution and a business contract between the company and the settlers—was signed in 1780, and the settlement was erected into the county of Davidson three years later.

Thus Richard Henderson may be credited with playing a major role in the beginning of two states—Kentucky and Tennessee.

Between his western trips, Henderson in 1778 was offered but declined appointment to the state's superior court (roughly comparable to the court on which he had sat five years earlier) and to the Council of State. After his return to North Carolina, he represented Granville County in the House of Commons in 1781, and the following year accepted appointment to the Council of State.

Richard Henderson married Elizabeth Keeling on December 28, 1763. Of their six children, two achieved special renown: Leonard Henderson became chief justice of the North Carolina Supreme Court, and Archibald Henderson served as a state legislator and congressman. Richard Henderson died at his home at Nutbush on January 30, 1785, and was buried in the family cemetery six miles north of present-day Henderson.

RICHARD HENDERSON

by Arthur Thomas

STEPHEN HOPKINS

[1707–1785]

by Bradford F. Swan

S TEPHEN HOPKINS, who signed the Declaration of Independence for Rhode Island in a hand shaky from the infirmities of old age but not from fear, was one of the American patriots whose influence was of great importance in bringing about the Revolution and, eventually, independence from Great Britain.

When the British armed customs vessel *Gaspee* was burned in Narragansett Bay in what has been claimed as the first act of overt violence against the crown in the American colonies, Hopkins was deeply involved. Born in what is now Cranston, Rhode Island, in 1707, he grew up on a farm in the country, and when that part of the state was organized as a town, Scituate, young Hopkins became the first town moderator. Self-educated, largely because there was little chance for formal education in the colony at that time, Hopkins moved to Providence while still a young man and became associated with some of the town's most influential merchants, like the Browns, in business and politics. Providence was then about half the size of Newport, which had dominated Rhode Island politics for nearly a century, but the town was on the rise and Hopkins's political influence rose with it.

When the *Gaspee* was burned Hopkins's relatives were involved and so were his business associates, the Browns. As chief justice of the superior court and as an influential member of the General Assembly, Hopkins chose to defy authority, and as a result the whole investigation failed to produce any culprits.

In 1764, when he was governor, Hopkins produced a pamphlet entitled *The Rights of Colonies Examined*. Although it did not bear his name, it has been well established that he was the author. This writing had immense influence, for although its general tone was one of calm detachment it challenged completely the right of the British Parliament to tax the colonists without their consent.

The pamphlet was reprinted throughout the colonies, mostly in newspapers, and had an enormous effect. It was also reprinted in the mother country, where it immediately drew several replies, including Samuel Johnson's *Taxation No Tyranny*. It was the Hopkins pamphlet that laid down the fundamental principle of no taxation without representation.

Within the colony of Rhode Island, however, Hopkins represented only one political party; the other, which had its power base in Newport and had formed an alliance with the South County "planters," was led by Samuel Ward. It is not strange, therefore, that when it came time to send delegates to the Continental Congress, political differences were set aside and the leaders of the two parties, Hopkins and Ward, were chosen. Ward fell ill and died before the Declaration was signed and William Ellery of Newport took his place and became the other signer from Rhode Island.

Hopkins barely survived the war. He died July 13, 1785. His influence on political thought in the American colonies in the years just before the Revolution cannot be overemphasized. Whereas the earliest complaints against the British authorities were based on economic grounds, that the laws promulgated in Britain hurt the colonists' business, he was able to move from this sort of thinking to the development of a position based on constitutional principles. It was this transition that brought about a sense of unity among the American colonies and led inevitably to independence.

STEPHEN HOPKINS

by James Reid Lambdin

JOHN EAGER HOWARD

[1752–1827]

by *Harold A. Williams*

J OHN EAGER HOWARD, a revolutionary soldier, was born on the Howard estate, Grey Rock, in Baltimore county, Maryland, June 4, 1752.

When the Revolution began, Howard, aged twenty-four, joined a body of militia and was commissioned a captain, June 25, 1776. Within two weeks he raised a company which was incorporated in a brigade of the Maryland Flying Camp fighting in New York. At the battle of White Plains, this force, with Howard in command of his company, covered the retreat of the Maryland line. On February 22, 1777, after a reorganization of the Maryland militia, Howard was commissioned a major in the Fourth Regiment. At the battle of Germantown, the commander was disabled by an accident and Howard assumed command. Howard and his troops wintered with Washington at Valley Forge and took part in the Battle of Monmouth. He was appointed lieutenant colonel and served under General Horatio Gates in the defeat at Camden by Cornwallis.

At the battle of Cowpens, January 17, 1781, an apparent American defeat was turned into an American victory. Much of the credit was given to Howard. His troops, which occupied the center of the American line, stood firm against a strong attack from Tarleton's British regulars. When the British, augmented by their reserves, pushed forward, Howard's men withdrew because of a misunderstood order. The position of the line was critical and the danger imminent because it threatened the Americans with defeat. But the withdrawal was orderly and Howard's men, after withstanding a third assault, charged with their bayonets in an open field. The battle showed that the Continentals could successfully fight

British regulars, and it raised drooping American spirits. Bancroft characterized the battle as the most astonishing victory of the war.

Howard also fought in the battles of Guilford Courthouse, Hobkirk's Hill, where he succeeded to command of the regiment, and Eutaw Springs, September 8, 1781, where he was wounded so severely that he was sent home. General Nathanael Greene, commander of the Southern Army, said of him, "He deserves a statue of gold no less than the Roman and Grecian heroes."

Howard was a delegate to the Continental Congress and served three terms of one year each as governor of Maryland (1788–91). He declined President Washington's offer to become secretary of war. In 1791 he was elected to the Maryland senate and in 1796 he was chosen to fill a vacancy in the United States Senate. He then was elected to serve a full term until 1803. He had married Peggy Oswald Chew, daughter of Chief Justice Benjamin Chew of Pennsylvania, May 18, 1787. They had four daughters and five sons, one of whom, George, was elected governor of Maryland.

A successful merchant and prominent landowner, Howard gave the city of Baltimore ground on which the Washington monument was built, land for the Lexington Market and a number of churches, including the Catholic cathedral. His military reputation is recalled in the lines of "Maryland, My Maryland." Maryland's Howard County is named for him and so are three Baltimore streets: John, Eager, and Howard. An equestrian statue in his honor stands near Baltimore's Washington monument. Howard died on October 12, 1827, at his estate Belvidere in Baltimore.

JOHN E. HOWARD

by Michael Laty after Charles Willson Peale

JAMES IREDELL

[1751–1799]

by Hugh Lefler

JAMES IREDELL, statesman and jurist, was born in England, October 5, 1751. His father, Francis Iredell, was a merchant in Bristol. His mother, Margaret McCulloh, was related to Henry McCulloh, one of the largest landowners in North Carolina. Iredell came to North Carolina when he was seventeen. He had just been appointed comptroller of the customs at Port Roanoke in Edenton, North Carolina.

Iredell was licensed to practice law in 1771. Two years later he began to speak and write on political questions. He entered into the discussion of points at issue between the colonies and England, taking "an advanced American position," but with no desire for separation from England. As late as June 1776, he was hopeful of reconciliation and peace. He rejected with disdain, until almost the last moment, the idea of American independence.

After the Revolution, Iredell was keenly interested in the establishment of a strong and effective federal government, and his pen gave able support to this cause. He wrote the Chowan County and Edenton Resolutions of November 8, 1787, which instructed their representatives in the General Assembly to vote for a convention to consider the Constitution.

After studying the Constitution carefully, Iredell published in January 1788, over the signature "Marcus," *Answers to Mr. Mason's Objections to the New Constitution*. This appeared serially in the *State Gazette of North Carolina* and was later published in pamphlet form. It attracted national attention and may have been a contributing factor in Washington's appointment of Iredell to the Supreme Court of the United States.

Perhaps the most significant work Iredell did in behalf of the Constitution was in the Hillsborough Convention of 1788, where he represented the borough of Edenton and was the floor leader of the Federalists, explaining and defending each section of the Constitution. His tact and good temper in a bad-tempered meeting contributed as much to enhance his reputation as his able arguments. The Anti-Federalists had a huge majority in the Convention and by a vote of 184 to 84 failed to ratify the Constitution.

Iredell published an address to the people of North Carolina in August 1788, warning them of the dangers of disunion. This essay protested the action of the Hillsborough Convention and pointed out the dangers arising from failure to ratify the Constitution.

The General Assembly which met in November 1788 was flooded with petitions urging a second convention, and by sizable majorities both houses adopted a resolution calling for a convention to meet at Fayetteville on November 16, 1789. This convention ratified the Constitution by a vote of 195 to 77.

On February 10, 1790, President Washington appointed Iredell associate justice of the United States Supreme Court. He was only thirty-eight, the youngest member on the bench. The functions of the justices at that time included holding the circuit courts. Iredell was assigned to the Southern Circuit, where he "led the life of a post boy in a circuit of vast extent, under great difficulties of travel and the perils of life in the sickly season."

As a constitutional lawyer, Iredell had no superior on the court, with the possible exception of James Wilson of Pennsylvania. All of his opinions are notable for their forcefulness.

The exhausting labor and continuous travel on the circuit undermined his health, and less than ten years after he had taken his seat on the bench, Iredell died at his home in Edenton, October 20, 1799. He is buried there.

JAMES IREDELL

Engraving by Albert Rosenthal

RALPH IZARD

[1742–1804]

by Shelby Foote

GRANDSON ON HIS FATHER'S SIDE of one of the colony's founders, whose namesake he was, and on his mother's of Robert Johnson, first governor under the crown, Ralph Izard was born at the Elms, the family estate near Charleston, South Carolina, in January 1742. His father died when he was seven, and five years later he was sent to school in England. He returned in 1764, aged twenty-two, to assume management of the extensive rice and indigo plantations he had inherited as an only son, and married within three years Alice De Lancey, niece of James De Lancey, former chief justice and lieutenant governor of New York. In 1771 he went to London, intending to remain there, and bought a house on fashionable Berners Street, where he and his wife indulged their fondness for the arts, especially literature and music, and the company of leading intellectuals of the day.

Tall and handsome—as evidenced in a portrait done by John Singleton Copley in Rome during a tour of the Continent in 1774—Izard was cultured, wealthy, and nothing if not aristocratic. Yet this outlook would seem to have operated downward rather than upward, so to speak, for he had already shown an alternate side of his nature by declining to be presented at court, on grounds of his unwillingness to "bow the knee . . . to mortal man." In any case, when he returned to England from the tour and found the Revolution heading up across the Atlantic, he did what he could to allay the crisis, in which his sympathies lay with the colonists, then moved his family to Paris in the fall of 1776, with the intention

[143]

of sailing home. Before he could do so in the following spring, however, he was informed that Congress had elected him commissioner to Tuscany.

Denied the chance to exercise his diplomatic talents in that direction by the refusal of the Tuscan government to receive him, he remained in Paris, and claimed the right to share in consultations between the French court and the ministers commissioned to it—a right not recognized by Benjamin Franklin, for whom Izard acquired an antipathy. It deepened with Franklin's refusal to pay his salary as commissioner to Tuscany out of funds collected in France or even to exempt his goods from duties in accordance with the privilege his appointment had conferred. Izard was ordered back to America in late 1779, his commission terminated.

Landing at Philadelphia in August 1780, he was pleased to learn that Congress, having studied his dispatches, had just passed a resolution approving his conduct. He then repaired to Washington's headquarters, where he rendered perhaps his greatest service to the cause by recommending Nathanael Greene as successor to Horatio Gates in command of the Southern Department. Two years later, back in South Carolina, he was elected to the Continental Congress, where he served until peace was declared the following year. Though he declined to run for governor, he was a member of the state legislature, and on the adoption of the federal Constitution in 1789 was elected to the U.S. Senate, where he became president *pro tempore* during the Third Congress.

A frequent sufferer from gout, which tended to make him increasingly and notoriously irascible down the years, he retired from public life in 1795 and two years later suffered a paralytic stroke that made him an invalid for the six years that were left him. Survived by his wife and seven of their fourteen children, he died near Charleston in 1804, aged sixty-two, and was buried, in accordance with his will, outside the wall of St. James Church, Goose Creek.

RALPH IZARD

by John Trumbull

JAMES JACKSON

[1757–1806]

by E. Merton Coulter

J A M E S J A C K S O N (September 21, 1757–March 19, 1806), was one of the most daring and resourceful soldiers of the Revolution in Georgia, entering his first military action when only seventeen. The highest rank he attained was lieutenant colonel of the famous "Jackson Legion," officially termed the "Georgia State Legion."

Jackson was born in Devonshire, England, and early showed his dislike for the British system of government by emigrating to Georgia, arriving in Savannah in 1772, where he studied law, but did not practice during the Revolution. In 1776, he joined a small force that attacked and set fire to British ships in the harbor; he helped seize the powder magazine there; and he joined the attack against British forces on Tybee Island, burned their headquarters, and drove them to their ships. Heading a force of light infantry, he participated in a campaign against the British marching up from Florida.

He took part in the unsuccessful defense of Savannah in 1778 against the attack of Archibald Campbell with an army of 2,000 men. Fleeing for safety, Jackson crossed the Savannah River into South Carolina and joined General William Moultrie's army, after having been mistaken for a spy and only at the last moment saved from being hanged. From this time on to the end of the war, he served with various commands throughout upper South Carolina and Georgia. In 1779, he joined the combined forces of General Benjamin Lincoln and comte d'Estaing in an unsuccessful attack to recover Savannah, showing great bravery.

Soon back in South Carolina, he joined the command of General Thomas

[147]

Sumter and took part in the battle of Blackstock's plantation against Colonel Banastre Tarleton's army. With General Nathanael Greene in command of the Southern Department, Jackson soon came to the favorable attention of Greene, especially after the resounding victory at Cowpens against Tarleton. In this battle, Jackson commanded the Georgia and South Carolina militia under General Daniel Morgan. Jackson's deploying his troops was crucial in winning the victory. After Cowpens, he joined in Greene's pursuit of Cornwallis into North Carolina. From 1781 on to the end, Jackson fought in Georgia, having initially organized the attack on Augusta that won the city that year. On Greene's recommendation, the Georgia legislature, in August of the same year, authorized the Jackson Legion; and General Anthony Wayne, now in command in Georgia, ordered Lieutenant Colonel Jackson to move southward and operate against the British in and around Savannah. With brilliancy and tenacity he penned the British up in that city, and when they capitulated on July 10, 1782, Wayne awarded Jackson the honor of the surrender.

Jackson's civil career after the war, much aided by his military service, gave him his larger place in American history, as governor of the state, United States congressman and senator. Basic in his political life was his opposition to the Yazoo Fraud, which related to the corrupt sale of the state's western territory, an area including most of the future states of Alabama and Mississippi, and he was one of the commissioners who effected the territory's transfer to the federal government, in 1802.

JAMES JACKSON

From a drawing by J. B. Longacre

[FROM CHARLES C. JONES, JR., "THE HISTORY OF GEORGIA"]

JOHN JAY

[1745–1829]

by *Richard B. Morris*

A<small>S</small> P<small>ATRIOT</small> and Founding Father, John Jay brought to his revolutionary commitment a deep concern for the national interest and a sense of justice, rooted in the English legal and constitutional system. In his long and distinguished public career, the New York lawyer held all the great posts of public service save the presidency of the new republic. In turn, he was chief justice of the state of New York, president of the Continental Congress, minister plenipotentiary to Spain during the American Revolution, a member of the peace commission that negotiated the treaty of 1783 with Great Britain recognizing American independence, secretary for foreign affairs in the Confederation years, and ad interim secretary of state under Washington before Jefferson assumed that office. While first chief justice of the United States, Jay negotiated the treaty with Great Britain of 1794 which bears his name, after which he served as a two-term governor of New York State.

A notable stylist and draftsman, Jay authored a number of state papers, including *The Address to the People of Great Britain* adopted by the first Continental Congress. Principal draftsman of the innovating New York Constitution of 1777, Jay made a significant contribution to the campaign for the ratification of the federal Constitution by participating with Hamilton and Madison in the writing of *The Federalist* and by his persuasive *Address to the New York State Convention*.

As a human being and negotiator, Jay could be austere, vain, rigid, and pertinacious. Inevitably his personality and activist role evoked criticism. He was criticized for bypassing the French court and entering into a separate preliminary peace with Great Britain in 1782 on the basis of information suggesting that the interests of his new nation could be better served thereby. He was criticized for proposing a compromise settlement with Spain over the navigation of the Mississippi and for negotiating a treaty with Great Britain in 1794 in which America seemed to yield more than it gained. In both negotiations Jay recognized the necessity of establishing a détente with two powerful nations at a time when the young United States was totally unprepared for war. As chief justice, Jay is associated with a cause célèbre, *Chisholm* v. *Georgia*, in which the Supreme Court held that states could be sued by private citizens, a doctrine quickly reversed by the Eleventh Amendment to the Constitution. More lasting were his decisions upholding the sanctity of treaties as the supreme law of the land. His opinions articulated on the bench foreshadowed the nationalist rulings of John Marshall.

Last of the members of the first Continental Congress to pass away, Jay lived a full life of eighty-four years, one enriched by cherished friendships, ennobled by unimpeachable integrity, and distinguished for his advocacy of humanitarian causes, of which freedom for the blacks was perhaps the most noteworthy. Appropriately Jay as governor signed the New York law he had long advocated providing for the emancipation of slaves in his state. Appropriately, his two sons, Peter Augustus and William, and his grandson, John Jay, were to be long identified as leaders of the abolition movement.

JOHN JAY

by Gilbert Stuart

NOBLE WIMBERLY JONES

[1723–1805]

by E. Merton Coulter

N OBLE WIMBERLY JONES (1723–January 9, 1805) was the "Morning Star of Liberty" in the revolutionary movement in Georgia. He was born near London and as a boy came to Georgia with his parents on the first ship to set up the colony under James Edward Oglethorpe, in 1733. He was a son of Noble Jones, of Welsh ancestry, and being taught by his physician father the practice of medicine, he continued in that profession to the end of his life. Oglethorpe appointed him a cadet in the Georgia Regiment, and although he did not long remain a soldier, he was active for a time against Indian depredations.

From the first the repressive measures of the British government met his opposition. He came into a position of leadership in 1755 when he was elected a member of the House of Assembly, where he served throughout the colonial period. He was elected speaker in 1768, and it was around this position that the forces of the Revolution gathered to oppose Governor James Wright. So distasteful had Jones's opposition to the governor become that Wright disallowed his election in 1771; and when Wright took a vacation in England (1771–73), he instructed James Habersham, who became the acting governor, to veto Jones's election if it came up again. At the beginning of the session in 1772, he was elected three successive times against Habersham's vetoes, resigning his third election so the house might function by electing a person less objectionable to the royal government.

Jones was one of the leaders against the Stamp Act and subsequently against all the British measures directed against the colonies. One of the issues around which there arose much bitterness was the appointment of the colonial agent to reside in London. In the course of this quarrel, Jones and his colleagues secured the appointment of Benjamin Franklin, who represented Georgia as well as Pennsylvania until the outbreak of war. Jones and Franklin became close friends.

The Lexington-Concord conflict created a furor in Georgia, which led to the organization of a group in Jones's house to seize the powder magazine. A provincial congress was soon held, which appointed Jones as one of the delegates to the second Continental Congress; but he did not attend out of respect to his dying father, who remained a loyalist.

Jones was elected speaker of the first House of Assembly under the state constitution of 1777. When the British captured Savannah, in 1778, Jones moved to Charleston, and when that city fell to the British, he was taken prisoner and sent to St. Augustine. In 1781, he was exchanged, but not allowed to return to Georgia.

He went to Philadelphia, became well acquainted with Dr. Benjamin Rush, and practiced medicine for a short time before being elected, by Georgia, a delegate to the Continental Congress. When the British surrendered Savannah in 1782, Jones returned. He was chairman of the reception committee that welcomed Washington to the city in 1791. Famous as a presiding officer, he was president of the Constitutional Convention of 1795, and when the Georgia Medical Society was organized in 1804, he became its first president. At the age of eighty-two he died, after an active practice that continued until a week before his death.

NOBLE W. JONES

by Charles Willson Peale

[WORMSLOE FOUNDATION, INC., SAVANNAH, GEORGIA]

WILLIE JONES

[1741–1801]

by Hugh Lefler

WILLIE JONES (pronounced Wylie Jones), revolutionary leader and "Father of Jeffersonian Democracy in North Carolina," was born in Surry County, Virginia, May 25, 1741, the son of Robin, Jr., and Sarah Cobb Jones. Sometime prior to 1753, the Joneses moved to Northampton County, North Carolina, settling about six miles from the town of Halifax.

Jones attended his father's alma mater, Eton, from 1753 to 1758, after which he made the grand tour of the Continent. When he returned to Halifax, he was described as a "peculiarly thoughtful and eccentric man." His home, the Grove, which he built at the southern end of town, became the center of social life and political activity for the region. He had one of the finest stables in the South and in 1790 owned one hundred and twenty slaves. On June 22, 1776, forsaking his vow of celibacy, he married the charming Mary Montfort. The couple had thirteen children. Only five of them lived to maturity and none lived to carry on the Jones name.

Between 1774 and 1775, he completely reversed his attitude about England's relationship to the colonies and became a convert to the Whig cause. Historians have long speculated as to why he changed his views. While an aristocrat in social life, Jones fervently believed in political democracy. He interpreted the struggle with Great Britain as a democratic movement and was determined to embody its revolutionary ideals in the government of the state and nation. His later opposition to the United States Constitution was inspired by his fear of a government that might become too powerful.

From the beginning of the quarrel with England he was an ardent supporter of colonial rights, and probably nothing else could have drawn him into politics. In 1774 he was recommended by the Board of Trade for a place on the colonial council but was not appointed because of his radical views. He served instead as chairman of the Halifax Committee of Safety. He supported the call for a provincial congress in 1774. This body remained in session for only three days, but during that time it fully launched North Carolina into the revolutionary movement. Jones was elected a member of each of the five provincial congresses, but he could not attend the fourth because the Continental Congress had appointed him superintendent of Indian affairs for the southern colonies. At the fifth provincial congress, with a liberal majority behind him, Jones served on the committee to draft the state constitution and bill of rights. He used his influence in shaping the state constitution. When it was completed, it was a compromise satisfactory to all but the conservative extremists.

During the next twelve years, Jones was politically the most powerful man in the state. He was a member of the House of Commons from 1777 to 1780, and a state senator for three terms between 1782 and 1788. In 1781 and 1787 he was a member of the Council of State. In 1780 he was elected to the Continental Congress and served one year.

Jones was elected a delegate to the federal Convention, but did not accept. When the Constitution was submitted to the state, he led the opposition to its ratification at the Hillsborough Convention of 1788. At this convention he wanted to adjourn the first day. He said, "all the delegates knew how they were going to vote," and he did not want to be guilty of "lavishing public money" on a long and tedious discussion in support of the Constitution and its immediate ratification in advance of amendment. After eleven days of debate, by a vote of 184 to 84, the Anti-Federalists carried a resolution neither rejecting nor ratifying the Constitution.

Jones favored a delay in ratification but public sentiment ran the other way. The Federalists carried on an effective campaign of education for a second convention to act on the Constitution. Jones was elected to the Convention of 1789, which met at Fayetteville and ratified the Constitution by a vote of 195 to 77, but he did not attend. His public career was over.

A street in Raleigh and a county in North Carolina bear Jones's name. He died in Raleigh after a long illness on June 8, 1801. At his own request, he is buried there in an unmarked grave.

WILLIE JONES

Engraving by Albert Rosenthal

JAMES ARMISTEAD
LAFAYETTE

[c1759–1830]

by *Ralph Ellison*

J A M E S   A R M I S T E A D, a slave, began his service with General Lafayette during 1781, when the young general was commanding forces pitted against General Cornwallis, to whose victory over General Gates in South Carolina many American slaves, who had joined the British on their promise of freedom, had contributed.

Trying desperately to raise four hundred laborers, teamsters, and badly needed cavalry mounts, Lafayette had advised Washington that "nothing but a treaty of alliance with the Negroes can find us dragoon Horses [because] it is by this means the enemy have so formidable a Cavalry." And it was during this period, with Cornwallis still formidable and the Americans badly in need of intelligence as to his strength and strategy, that James Armistead sought his master's permission to join Lafayette.

His owner consenting, Armistead enlisted and served the future hero of the French Revolution so effectively that after the war the general was to state that his spying activities were "industriously collected and more faithfully delivered." Armistead had carried out important commissions so effectively that the general recommended him as worthy of "every reward his situation could admit of."

The brevity of Lafayette's testimonial understated his intelligent agent's resourcefulness. Taking advantage of the British eagerness for Negro aid, Armistead had risked his life by pretending to supply Cornwallis with information damaging to the Americans—a bit of playacting so perfectly performed that not until the defeated Cornwallis encountered him in Lafayette's headquarters was the black man's true loyalty and identity revealed.

The rest is irony. In 1786, Armistead, who by now expressed his continuing admiration for the marquis by calling himself James Armistead Lafayette, was rewarded for his services to the Revolution by being emancipated at the expense of the General Assembly of Virginia. In 1818, still free, but little changed in circumstance, the old ex-spy successfully petitioned the state for relief, acquiring after thirty years a veteran's pension.

The essential incongruity of his position was, however, unchanged. Although a recognized veteran of the Revolution and a free man, he was not a citizen. He had, nevertheless, emerged somewhat from the shadow in which he had stood in earlier years. And in 1824, during Lafayette's visit to Virginia, Armistead's now aging features were to share once more the general's glory.

John B. Martin, an artist as skilled in delineating a revolutionary veteran who was an ex-slave and spy as one who became chief justice of the Supreme Court (John Marshall), painted Armistead's portrait. Proud and dignified, he appears with his highly individualized features forcefully drawn, a dark, ruggedly handsome man looking out at the viewer with quizzical expression. He wears a white neckcloth, his blue military coat bearing no medals is simply adorned with bright buttons embossed with the American eagle. Asserting an individual identity earned at the repeated risk of his life, James Armistead Lafayette affirmed an unshakable faith in the ideal of democracy. His portrait now hangs in the Valentine Museum at Richmond.

JAMES LAFAYETTE

by John B. Martin

[VALENTINE MUSEUM, RICHMOND, VIRGINIA]

MARQUIS DE LAFAYETTE

[1757–1834]

by Clifford K. Shipton

BORN INTO A FAMILY of the ancient nobility, Marie Joseph Paul Yves Roch Gilbert du Motier de Lafayette (1757–1834) early lost his father and inherited a substantial fortune. Following family tradition, he joined the army, and was serving on the Rhine when he was charmed by the account given by the duke of Gloucester of the goals and struggles of the American rebels. Most of his family tried to dampen his enthusiasm, but with the aid of his uncle, the marquis de Noailles, the French ambassador at London, he made his way to America. Between him and the childless George Washington there sprang up such an attachment as usually exists only between father and son. He was brave and his military service was adequate, and he swallowed his chagrin when it was proposed as a hoax that he lead an invasion of Canada in 1778. While d'Estaing was at Rhode Island, Lafayette gave invaluable service as liaison officer. Returning to France in 1780, he joined in the preparation of the Rochambeau expedition. Coming back to America ahead of it, he suffered agonies lest this elegant army arrive to find that the tattered American forces had melted away during the winter. He was vindicated when his aristocratic colleagues saw the idealism beyond the rags of the Americans. He served creditably during the closing campaigns of the war.

Returning to France, Lafayette became the voice of American-style democracy. He did his best to move the French Revolution in that direction. It was he who designed the red, white, and blue flag of the French Republic in the hope that it would symbolize the moderation of the revolution. In that he failed. He was jailed by the radicals, broke with Napoleon, and sat out the remaining years of the war. In 1824 at the invitation of President Monroe he returned to tour the United States for a year, and was welcomed as though he were all the heroes of the Revolution rolled into one.

MARQUIS de LAFAYETTE

by Charles Willson Peale

RICHARD HENRY LEE

[1732–1794]

by *Merrill D. Peterson*

I N   T H E   A N N A L S of the American Revolution no family is more eminent than the Lees of Virginia, and Richard Henry Lee is the brightest star in the galaxy. Born in 1732 at the ancestral home Stratford, one of six sons in the fourth Virginia generation of the family, Lee entered the House of Burgesses in 1758 and gradually rose to prominence as a leader, second only to Patrick Henry, of the insurgent popular party against the conservative oligarchy in Williamsburg. To these men he seemed a traitor to his class, and he earned their enmity by helping to expose a massive scandal in the colonial treasury. At the same time, in 1765–66, he and other "young hot-heads," as the governor labeled them, boldly challenged the local magnates by their uncompromising opposition to Parliament's Stamp Act. In his own county Lee organized the Westmoreland Association, the first system of economic boycott against the mother country, which would later be applied colony-wide and finally to the entire continent.

Lee was among the first Americans to call for a continental congress in order to form a united resistance against Britain after the passage of the Intolerable Acts of 1774. When the Congress met at Philadelphia, Lee and Henry, among the Virginia delegates, promptly distinguished themselves by the brilliance of their oratory. They were imaged for all time as the Cicero and the Demosthenes of the Revolution.

A tall, slender man, with a thin face, pensive eyes, high receding brow, reddish hair, and a captivating musical voice, Lee seemed to many, as he did to John Adams, "a masterly man." The collaboration between the Virginian and the

Massachusetts "brace of Adamses," John and Samuel, in 1774 gave rise to the so-called Lee-Adams Junto, which spearheaded the movement for independence. It was Lee who, on June 7, 1776, offered the resolution that the united colonies "are, and of right ought to be, free and independent states." Congress adopted the epoch-making resolution on July 2, but the fame that might have gone to its author was eclipsed by the Declaration of Independence adopted two days later.

From the pinnacle of American independence, Lee's career followed a descending and uncertain course. Early a champion of the French alliance, he became embroiled in his brother Arthur's controversy with Benjamin Franklin's ministry in Paris and turned hostile to France. Early a radical in Virginia politics, he later allied himself with conservative elements in the state. Early, and always, a strong unionist, he nevertheless opposed the movement for a national government and enrolled himself at the head of the Anti-Federalists against the adoption of the Constitution. The new government, he feared, would usurp the rights of citizens and states and grow tyrannical. Finally, he agreed to support it if his first demand, the addition of a bill of rights, could be met. Virginia elected him to the U.S. Senate where he continued the fight for a bill of rights. In 1792, after the first ten amendments were ratified, Lee resigned his seat, retired in broken health to his modest estate Chantilly, on the Potomac, and died two years later.

RICHARD HENRY LEE

by Charles Willson Peale

[INDEPENDENCE NATIONAL HISTORICAL PARK COLLECTION, PHILADELPHIA]

JAMES MADISON

[1751–1836]

by Irving Brant

JAMES MADISON (1751–1836), fourth president of the United States, is best known as "the father of the Constitution"—a document that he himself said "ought to be regarded as the work of many minds and many hands." Educated at the College of New Jersey (now Princeton), he spent his next nine years battling successfully for freedom of religion in Virginia and promoting colonial resistance to England. His four years in the Continental Congress led the French minister to write that he was "regarded as the man of the soundest judgment" in that body. In it he stood for national supremacy, sought congressional taxing power, defended American territorial claims, and established national ownership of western lands.

Instrumental in summoning the 1787 Constitutional Convention, Madison charted its course with a Virginia Plan that embodied the basic principles and structure of the new government. His "Notes of Debates" furnish the history of that convention. He took the lead, wrote another delegate, "in the management of every great question." In the battle for ratification by Virginia, Madison overcame the mighty orator Patrick Henry, leading Chief Justice John Marshall to say, in retrospect, that "If eloquence is the art of persuading by convincing, James Madison was the most eloquent man I have ever heard."

In the U.S. House of Representatives (1789–97) Madison produced the first ten amendments to the Constitution, fought for justice to unpaid revolutionary veterans, sought to counter discriminatory British navigation acts, and laid the groundwork of Jeffersonian Democracy. Retiring to Montpelier with his wife

Dolley, he drafted the Virginia Resolutions denying the constitutionality of the Alien and Sedition Acts.

As President Jefferson's secretary of state (1801–9) Madison directed the strategy that produced the purchase of the Louisiana Territory. For eight years he and Jefferson worked to uphold American maritime rights while keeping out of the Napoleonic Wars. Nominated for president in 1808, he won the election by publication of his diplomatic dispatches disproving the charge of subservience to Bonaparte.

Desiring peace but intent on maintaining American rights, Madison's first action as president was to notify warring England and France that cessation by one country of its depredations on American commerce, if not followed by similar action by the other belligerent, would lead to war against the continuing offender. After long negotiations, this led to the War of 1812. In that war, brilliant American naval exploits and American defeats on land were followed in 1814 by successive victories by American armies. With New England in near revolt against the war, Madison's firm adherence to civil liberties thwarted secession movements. The outcome, construed in Europe as an American triumph, produced national harmony and international prestige.

During Madison's post-presidential years (1817–36) world travelers and American statesmen frequented Montpelier. His last seven years were spent in ceaseless battle against southern nullification and secession. A slaveowner by economic compulsion, Madison sought to free the slaves by government purchase and manumission. Never a church member, he supported "liberal Christianity" and expressed "his own regard for the Unitarian doctrine." His outstanding qualities were intellectual insight and incorruptible integrity.

JAMES MADISON

by Gilbert Stuart

[BOWDOIN COLLEGE MUSEUM OF ART, BRUNSWICK, MAINE]

FRANCIS MARION

[1732–1795]

by W. Edwin Hemphill

H E W A S A W I Z E N E D R U N T of a man but hardy and energetic, capable of sleeping on the ground without benefit of blanket or tent. And, in a generation that detested Hessians and other "mercenaries" or professional soldiers, this second-generation Huguenot of South Carolina's Low Country personified perfectly the revolutionary ideal of the self-reliant yeoman who was willing to take up arms in defense of his home for the public welfare.

Little is known about his first forty years. Not even the place and date of his birth—probably in Saint John's Parish, Berkeley County, South Carolina, in 1732—are matters of record. Enlistment as a private in the Cherokee campaign of 1760–61 interrupted briefly his farming life there. From bucolic obscurity he stepped in 1775 into service in the colony's first revolutionary convention, its provincial congress. When that body organized two regiments, he was elected to be a captain in the second. He helped it on June 28, 1776, to repulse the British fleet from Charleston harbor and thus relieved the southern colonies of major military pressures for two years.

Dull discipline in the Charleston area followed; Marion excelled in the unspectacular routine of organization and training. He became the chief architect of the Second Regiment. In Continental and militia service he advanced to the rank of brigadier general. In September 1779, he participated in the ill-managed, disastrous campaign against the British in Savannah; but he protested against that assault upon an entrenched enemy and argued that swiftness of maneuver would have forestalled that mistake.

Marion's fame rests largely upon his quick, elusive movements during fourteen months of 1780–81. Commanding a flexible force of only a few hundred men, at most, and sometimes of only a score or two, he proved himself to be a master of guerrilla warfare. Singlehandedly he suppressed Tories and held the British at bay in the South Carolina lowlands, then helped "Light Horse Harry" Lee to capture British posts along the Santee, and commanded a corps in the army with which Nathanael Greene drove the British from the state. The frustrated Banastre Tarleton dubbed Marion the Swamp Fox, exclaiming that the devil himself could not catch him.

The Continental Congress expressed thanks to this brigadier general "of the South Carolina Militia for his wise, gallant and decided conduct," particularly for "his prudent and intrepid attack" against redcoats at Parker's Ferry and for his "distinguished part" in the Battle of Eutaw Springs on September 8, 1781. All told, Marion had probably never marched or ridden as much as two hundred miles from his home, but in the distinctive southern operations he had been indispensable in the prelude to victory at Yorktown.

His remaining years, the fourteen until his death in 1795, were prosaic but constructive. Marion was left by the war with little but his land; so South Carolina conferred upon its outstanding militiaman a command at Charleston in the 1780s but reduced its stipend when he married a wealthy Huguenot spinster. She bore him no children. As a state senator during 1782–86 (and again during 1791–94), he advocated conspicuously lenient, rather than vindictive, measures against South Carolinians who had been British sympathizers. That stance was in harmony with his invariable courtesy, his dignity spiced with occasional flashes of keen humor, and his humane disposition. He served as a member of the convention that much improved in 1790 his state's first constitution.

Francis Marion was essentially a plain, useful man. But events vouchsafed to him—and he richly earned—one brief interlude of glory. His tactical genius, founded upon thoroughness in preparation, unswerving patriotism, and purity of character, enabled him to respond brilliantly when extraordinary services were possible.

FRANCIS MARION

Print after a painting
by John Blake White

GEORGE MASON

[1725–1792]

by Alistair Cooke

T O A L L B U T his most intimate friends, George Mason (1725–92) must
have appeared to be almost grotesquely miscast as a revolutionary. He was
born to landed wealth, reared by private tutors, and had the run of a distinguished private library from boyhood on. When he came of age, he inherited five
thousand acres on the Potomac and brought over an indentured Oxford architect
to design his mansion, where he married happily, fathered five sons and four
daughters, ran his plantation without a steward, never tired of bemoaning the
"chatterers" who ran public affairs, and had every intention of living out his
days as a vestryman, justice of the peace, and "a private gentleman." And so, to
everyone outside Virginia, he seemed to be, until he accepted his first public
office by claiming a seat at the Constitutional Convention in 1787. He was then
sixty-two years old.

But his disdain for "the busy conduct of public affairs" was an affectation,
quite possibly a mark of envy in a chronic invalid, and was joshingly tolerated by
his few intimates. He is very close to a type still extant, and far more common in
England than in this country: the aristocratic farmer (Leicester of Holkham
Hall?), the retiring Oxford don (Isaiah Berlin?), who is later seen to have influenced men who were at the center of events. Mason, brooding in his library over
civil rights or the future of the Northwest Territory, was in close touch by correspondence with George Washington. He was the lonely champion in the East
of George Rogers Clark's hardy campaigns in the West. He can fairly be said to
be the intellectual father of the independence of Virginia.

When the Revolution was brewing, he wrote, from the pleasant shade of his acres, letters to London merchants summarizing with brilliant gravity the mood and arguments of the colonists. The closing of the port of Boston prompted him to draft a paper, known as the Fairfax Resolves, that was accepted "in toto" by the first Continental Congress as its basic constitutional position against the crown. On the outbreak of war, he framed a declaration of rights for the Constitution of Virginia that amounted to the model for the federal Bill of Rights.

Sitting among the Founding Fathers in Philadelphia, he constantly thrashed over the "babblers" who "so ill-conducted" the great cause. But when "a few weighty members began to take the lead," he was one of them. He could not overcome a strong alliance of New England shippers and slaveowners from the Deep South, and his clause prohibiting slavery was stricken from the emerging Constitution. His bitterness was aggravated by his failure to override Hamilton's argument that "the Constitution is itself . . . a bill of rights" in which "individual rights are inborn and presumed." He retired to Virginia to battle for the rejection of the Constitution, and lost by 89 to 79. But the hullabaloo he had caused was renewed, most prominently by Jefferson, and the written Bill of Rights came to be.

Mason was an improbable variation on the type of the liberal gadfly, often so irritating to comfortable people. But such people are necessary scourges to the public conscience. Without them, we might still have child labor or be conducting our holy mission in Vietnam. Mason made a constant nuisance of himself, and, in so doing, reaffirmed in print, and in the courts, the liberties we are sworn to live by.

GEORGE MASON

by D. W. Boudet

ROBERT MORRIS

[1734–1806]

by Irving Brant

R OBERT MORRIS, rightly known as the Financier of the American Revolution, was born in England on January 6, 1734, and joined his father in Maryland at the age of thirteen. He attended school briefly in Philadelphia and worked there for a well-established trading, navigating, and banking firm which became Willing, Morris and Company, and he rose to a partnership in it at the age of twenty. It was an almost lifelong connection.

In 1765 Morris signed the Philadelphia merchants' nonimportation agreement against England and joined in resisting the British Stamp Act. Stirred to revolution by the Battle of Lexington, he was appointed to the Pennsylvania Council of Safety, for which he became a procurer of military supplies from Europe. Later in 1775 his firm entered into a contract with the Continental Congress for that same purpose. In November the Pennsylvania Assembly elected him to Congress. That body appointed him to the Committee of Secret Correspondence with American agents in Europe. He immediately took leadership in the importation of arms and ammunition and establishment of national credit.

In 1776 Morris stood with his state's delegation in seeking to delay the Declaration of Independence "to let the laggard states catch up," but was the first of nine Pennsylvanians to sign the Declaration after the assembly's hampering instructions were revoked. His firm received commissions on purchases of European supplies, but he employed and risked his entire large fortune by furnishing private credit for public transactions.

The state's three-year constitutional limit forced Morris out of office on November 1, 1778. Five days later he entered the Pennsylvania Assembly. In Congress belated charges of financial improprieties led, at his request, to an examination of his books. The examining committee reported that he "has acted with fidelity and integrity and an honorable zeal for the happiness of his country." By 1781—three years later—the military situation was critical, Continental currency had collapsed, specie loans by France were absorbed by earlier congressional drafts on the French Treasury. In desperation Congress scrapped rule by committee and turned to Robert Morris for salvation. By unanimous vote he was elected superintendent of finance.

Morris promptly induced Congress to create the highly useful Bank of North America, with power to borrow money and emit legal tender notes. Currency was stabilized, credit vastly improved, but Arthur Lee's antibank, anti-French faction furiously assailed Morris. James Madison spearheaded his defense. Morris, Madison believed, accepted office from honorable and patriotic motives. There had been "no proof of misfeasance." Many charges were "palpably erroneous"; others, "somewhat suspicious, vanish on examination." They came from "known and vindictive enemies." The investigating committee found that Morris had conducted his business "with great ability and assiduity, and in a manner highly advantageous to the United States."

In 1787 Morris helped draft the new federal Constitution, taking no recorded part in debate but working to create a strong national government. Late in his life, Europe's economic collapse in the Napoleonic Wars paralyzed Morris's large-scale western lands speculations and wiped out his great fortune. Barbaric American law sent him to debtor's prison for three years but did not diminish the nation's debt to him for revolutionary services surpassed only by those of General Washington.

ROBERT MORRIS

by Charles Willson Peale

[INDEPENDENCE NATIONAL HISTORICAL PARK COLLECTION, PHILADELPHIA]

JAMES OTIS

[1725–1783]

by Samuel Eliot Morison

JAMES OTIS, "the Patriot," was born February 5, 1725, eldest of thirteen children, to Mary Allyne and Colonel James Otis, at Barnstable, Massachusetts. Graduated from Harvard in 1743, he read law, was admitted to the bar, moved to Boston, and married Ruth Cunningham. An excellent classical and legal scholar (he published a treatise on Latin prosody in 1760), as barrister his mind was supple, his apprehension quick, his pleading brilliant and captivating. Governor Hutchinson, his future enemy, admitted that "he never knew a fairer or more noble conduct in a pleader." His reputation was made by an argument in February 1761 against the issuance of writs of assistance to support Parliament's revenue laws. As John Adams, who was present, later recalled, "Otis was a flame of fire . . . American independence was then and there born." And Adams's notes on Otis's argument contain this significant sentence: "An act against the Constitution is void; an act against natural equity is void." This insistence that fundamental or natural laws were superior to acts of Parliament later became embodied in the federal and state constitutions, evolving into the American doctrine of courts having power to void constitutional laws.

The 1761 argument thrust Otis into local politics; he and Samuel Adams became leaders of the legislative opposition to the royal governors. In 1762 he wrote *A Vindication of the Conduct of the House of Representatives;* and in 1764, *The Rights of the British Colonies Asserted and Proved.* These two presented basic Whig theory of the British constitution clearly, forcefully, and in a brilliant style which made them basic handbooks for the patriot party. In 1765 he represented

[191]

Massachusetts Bay at the New York Stamp Act Congress, where he met Whig leaders of other colonies, such as Thomas McKean and John Dickinson of Pennsylvania, who were impressed by his learning and wit.

Otis had already shown signs of mental instability, such as excessive irritability, passionate overstatement, and unwonted vehemence in debate; but he always opposed public violence and mob rule. He was, therefore, stirred to a frenzy of resentment when some intercepted letters showed that the royal officials in Massachusetts had denounced him as a malignant incendiary. He posted them as liars, and at a coffeehouse brawl in 1769, one of them struck him a blow on the head which, although far from lethal, seems to have played a leading part in permanently unhinging his reason. Although he continued to plead in the courts, he gradually dropped out of public life. Declared *non compos mentis* in 1771 and placed under the guardianship of a younger brother, he lived quietly until May 23, 1783 when he was struck dead by a bolt of lightning while he was watching a thunderstorm.

As a political leader Otis was too violent and erratic to have much effect; but his well-thought-out pamphlets did much to lay the intellectual foundation of the American cause.

JAMES OTIS

From the original painting by
Alonzo Chappel

CHARLES WILLSON PEALE

[1741–1827]

by *Charles Coleman Sellers*

ANNAPOLIS WAS A formative influence in this life—a gay little provincial capital dominated by the easygoing moods and intellectual independence of Maryland's plantation aristocracy. Charles Willson Peale (1741–1827) thought of himself as a gentleman-born and yet, eldest son of a poor widow, grew up as an apprentice and tradesman with a compulsive liking for hard work that never left him. He dabbled in poetry, then turned painter. Immensely proud of his Huguenot grandmother, he learned her language, read Rousseau, Montesquieu, and other of the new libertarian French writers whose works were in the libraries of his more well-to-do friends. Some of those friends sent him to London to study art with Benjamin West. In London he worked hard as ever, stoutly refused to doff his hat as the king's coach rumbled by, and for his masterwork of those years, painted a huge piece of William Pitt in Roman costume, championing the liberties of America. He came home in 1769, with that painting warmly praised by the Virginia gentlemen who had commissioned it.

This was the making of one of those revolutionaries who threw themselves heart and soul into the struggle when it came, and yet to whom the war was only a preliminary episode. America, liberated, guided by reason and humanity, would set an example of enlightened civilization, a New World standard for all the world to follow. Peale moved with his family to Philadelphia, where John Adams met him in 1776, praised his paintings and described the painter to Abigail as a "tender, affectionate creature." So he was and so remained, a captain in the arduous Philadelphia campaigns from Trenton to Valley Forge, mothering his men,

[195]

making them shoes, finding them forage and rest—an artist gone to war with rifle at his back, sword and paint box together at his side.

His baptism by fire was at Princeton, a wintry dawn after that long night march, and his full-length portrait of Washington, commissioned by the state of Pennsylvania at the close of the campaign, shows the field as he remembered it when the firing ended and cheering began—the college buildings, the redcoated prisoners guarded by men in blue. He had painted Washington as a provincial colonel seven years before, again in 1776, and later life portraits followed, but this one, repeated in many replicas, has a character all its own. Portraits of other leaders came with it, among them the French allies, Lafayette and others who had become his friends.

After Valley Forge, eager to participate in the making of the new nation, Peale entered politics and held a seat in the Pennsylvania legislature that passed America's first act for the emancipation of slaves—all the while publicizing the glories of France and America in allegorical paintings. After Yorktown, he enlarged his studio into a portrait gallery of the heroes of American independence, and, four years later, expanded it again into a museum of natural history.

That museum became a life work. Nature, and a right knowledge of it, he now saw as key to the America of the poets and philosophers, the America of which he had dreamed. Natural history, well taught, would dispel all the superstitious clutter inherited from past ages, and a great era of healthful and peaceful living ensue. That was a dream, but the artist's life work remains in more than a thousand portraits of men and women who had in one way or another shared it with him—an enduring human record of climactic years.

CHARLES WILLSON PEALE

by Charles Willson Peale

[PENNSYLVANIA ACADEMY OF THE FINE ARTS]

DAVID RITTENHOUSE

[1732–1796]

by Henry Steele Commager

"YOU MUST REMEMBER," wrote Jefferson to his friend David Rittenhouse, "that the world has but one Ryttenhouse, and that it never had one before." The famous Dr. Benjamin Rush, a Philadelphia associate who knew Rittenhouse well, was equally laudatory. Rittenhouse was, he said, "one of the luminaries of the century." And so he was. Over in Germany the celebrated Christoph Ebeling asserted that Rittenhouse was the greatest of American astronomers, up in Birmingham Dr. Priestley sang his praises, and the Royal Society —rather late in the day, to be sure—conferred on him the ultimate accolade of membership. Rittenhouse himself was president of that sister institution, the American Philosophical Society, but here his just fame was overshadowed by the greater fame of his predecessor, Dr. Franklin, and his successor, Mr. Jefferson. With Franklin, James Logan, John Bartram, Dr. Rush, and his own nephew Benjamin Smith Barton, Rittenhouse made Philadelphia the scientific and cultural center of the New World. As with most of these men—the pattern is so common one suspects the operation of a Philadelphia standard—he played a distinguished role in public as well as in the intellectual life of his community; like most of them, too, he combined theory and practice, provincialism and cosmopolitanism, specialization with versatility, and a strong strain of romanticism with the spirit of the Enlightenment.

The son of a Pennsylvania farmer, Rittenhouse was almost wholly self-educated; while still a boy he taught himself mathematics and mastered Newton's *Principia.* He earned his living as a clockmaker and a kind of scientific handyman.

[199]

For George Washington he made spectacles, and for the College of Philadelphia an orrery which reproduced the operation of all the bodies in the solar system for five thousand years—a work of science and of art which elicited from Jefferson the tribute that "Mr. Rittenhouse has not indeed made a world, but he has by imitation approached nearer its Maker than any man who has ever lived from the day of creation to this day." He constructed his own observatory too, and ground his own telescope, and in 1769, along with astronomers from seven different countries with all their panoply of sophisticated apparatus, he traced the transit of Venus. His observations compared favorably with those of the Royal Observatory at Greenwich—except for an interval of some sixty seconds when he was apparently overcome with ecstasy at what he saw. Increasingly involved in public affairs, Rittenhouse was faithful to mathematics and astronomy to the end of his life; as late as the 1790s he was tracing the transit of Mercury, observing lunar eclipses, and in 1793 he discovered a new comet.

Meantime he displayed that versatility characteristic of the Enlightenment and especially of the American Enlightenment. He was one of the nation's most skillful surveyors, fixing the boundaries of parts of Pennsylvania, New York, and Massachusetts, and he conducted surveys for the new canals that were being constructed everywhere in the North. He inspected the first steam engine in America and approved of John Fitch's steamboat, which anticipated that of Robert Fulton by two decades. He served as professor of astronomy at the university and as trustee of that institution, too; he was librarian of the American Philosophical Society and then its president. From the outbreak of hostilities with the mother country he was an ardent patriot. He supervised the casting of cannon and the installation of the great iron chain to bar a British naval attack on Philadelphia; he was a member of the state assembly and of the Constitutional Convention of 1776; president of the State Council of Safety, member of the Board of War, and treasurer of the state. Washington appointed him the first director of the U.S. Mint; it was a position similar to that which Isaac Newton had held at the end of his life. As he was dying, Rittenhouse read Pascal and Rousseau; it was symbolic of a life embracing orthodoxy and heterodoxy, convention and revolution.

DAVID RITTENHOUSE

by Charles Willson Peale

CAESAR RODNEY

[1728–1784]

by *Jenkin Lloyd Jones*

THERE HAVE BEEN great events so much in the balance that a speck of dust falling upon one side would tilt the scale. And what may have saved the American nation at the very hour of its birth was the ride of a mud-spattered and exhausted man who tied up his lathered horse and hurried painfully into Independence Hall in Philadelphia on the late afternoon of July 2, 1776.

Two days later he wrote home, simply: "I arrived in Congress (though detained by thunder and rain) in time enough to give my vote to the matter of independence. It is determined by the 13 United Colonies, without even one dissenting vote. . . . Don't neglect to attend closely to my harvest and you'll oblige. Yours, etc.—Caesar Rodney."

Caesar Rodney, squire of Poplar Grove farm near Dover, Delaware, was described by John Adams as "the oddest looking man I ever saw—tall, slender as a reed, pale; his face is not bigger than a large apple, yet there is a sense and fire, spirit, wit and humor in his countenance."

It was a face that was to know horror, for a slow-spreading cancer progressively disfigured it for ten years and killed him in 1784 at the age of fifty-five. But of his fire and spirit there was no question.

At thirty-six he was a delegate to the Stamp Act Congress. Three years later he helped write a protest to the king over the Townshend Act. In the spring of 1774, after Parliament passed the Boston Port Bill, he put his neck in a noose as speaker of the Delaware colonial legislature by calling it into special session.

He, Thomas McKean, and George Read were chosen to represent Delaware in the Continental Congresses.

On June 6, 1776, when Richard Henry Lee electrified (and frightened) the second Congress with his demand that "these United States are, and ought to be, free and independent" the confusion following the 7 to 6 approval was so great that a three-weeks' recess was called.

A breathing spell—a time for contemplation and resolution—was vital, for the separatists realized that a mere majority vote for a new nation would not be enough, that a declaration must be unanimous if it were to have moral force. Rodney hurried home to overawe a rising of the Tories and to cajole the Delaware assembly into denying the authority of the crown.

On July 1 confusion still reigned in Philadelphia. Just nine colonies supported independence. New York's delegates had been instructed to abstain. Pennsylvania and South Carolina had dissented. And McKean and Read, acting for Delaware, had split yes and no.

In the feverish hours that followed, the nay-sayers in the Pennsylvania group agreed to absent themselves. South Carolina changed its mind. New York would not object. And an "express" from McKean reached Rodney at his farm just as he was retiring. Only he could tip Delaware.

It is still eighty miles from Dover to Independence Hall, but today it is a ninety-minute breeze on the four lanes. Rodney spurred his horse through a succession of quagmires on a rutted trail in a black night of storm. And out of the storm came the vote that made it possible to claim that, of all thirteen colonies assembled, not one would stay in the empire.

Paul Revere had a great press agent—Henry Wadsworth Longfellow. Caesar Rodney had no press agent, nor was he tuned to romantic imagery. But Longfellow's line, "The fate of a nation was riding that night," could better have been applied to the muddy gentleman from Delaware who dashed to Philadelphia.

RODNEY CASTING HIS VOTE IN INDEPENDENCE HALL JULY 4,1776

"AS I BELIEVE THE VOICE OF MY CONSTITUENTS AND OF ALL
SENSIBLE AND HONEST MEN IS IN FAVOR OF INDEPENDENCE, MY
OWN JUDGMENT CONCURS WITH THEM, I VOTE FOR INDEPENDENCE"

CAESAR RODNEY

by James E. Kelly

[HISTORICAL SOCIETY OF DELAWARE]

BENJAMIN RUSH

[1746–1813]

by Michael E. DeBakey, M.D.

"HE AIMED WELL" was Benjamin Rush's own assessment of himself, included among his character sketches of the signers of the Declaration of Independence. But he was more than a good aimer. Though a physician by profession, and often called the father of American psychiatry, he had a consuming interest in diverse disciplines and activities. In addition to being a heroic physician, he was a brilliant teacher, ardent patriot, humanitarian reformer, loving husband, and devoted father.

Born January 4, 1746, in Byberry, Pennsylvania, Rush attended a private academy and then matriculated at the College of New Jersey at Princeton, from which he received the bachelor of arts degree in 1760. He was strongly attracted to theology but chose a career in medicine. After serving six years as a medical apprentice to Dr. John Redman, he entered the University of Edinburgh, where he received his medical education. He graduated in 1768, and then worked in London hospitals and visited Paris before returning to Philadelphia to begin medical practice in 1769. About a year after the death of his former fiancée, Sarah Eve, Rush married Julia Stockton, seventeen years his junior. She bore him thirteen children, nine of whom lived to adulthood. Rush held the first chair of chemistry in America and, after twenty years in this position, became professor of medicine at the University of Pennsylvania, a post which he held until his death from typhus on April 19, 1813.

Rush built a tremendous private practice, partly as a result of his profuse medical publications on topics ranging from military hygiene to psychiatry. His professional standing was also enhanced by the large number of students and apprentices whom he taught, estimated at about three thousand during his tenure. A radical among physicians, he theorized that all diseases are really one—due to a fever caused by overstimulation of the blood vessels. His remedy was simple: "depletion" by bloodletting and purges, to which he himself submitted when he contracted yellow fever in the epidemic of 1793. His contributions to psychiatry were more impressive. Believing that insanity often developed from physical disorders and insisting that it was a disease rather than that the insane were possessed of the devil, he advocated humane treatment and worked for many years with the insane patients at Pennsylvania Hospital.

A versatile and influential figure of his times, Rush was active in the American Revolution, serving first in the provincial congress and then in the Continental Congress, where, with the other members, he signed the Declaration of Independence. From 1776 to 1778 he served as Continental physician general.

After the Revolution Rush labored incessantly to accomplish social and political reforms. He believed that with the end of the War of Independence the American Revolution had just begun, and he directed his energies to changing the "principles, opinions, and manners" of the times to accommodate them to the new republican government. He wrote voluminously, attacking slavery, "spirituous liquors," tobacco, war, and the penal system, and advocating free public schools, education of women, and establishment of a national university.

For thirty-seven years until his death, Benjamin Rush shared a tender relationship with his wife, "dear" Julia, whom he considered the "faithful companion of his pains and pleasures." Throughout his married life he turned to her for comfort and support. His devotion to his children is probably best understood by the anguish he suffered with quiet courage because of the mental illness of one of them.

The words of his cherished friend, John Adams, upon the death of Benjamin Rush, perhaps best sum up the manner of this man: "As a man of Science, Letters, Taste, Sense, Phylosophy, Patriotism, Religion, Morality, Merit, Usefulness, taken alltogether Rush has not left his equal in America, nor that I know in the World."

BENJAMIN RUSH

by Thomas Sully

[AMERICAN PHILOSOPHICAL SOCIETY]

HAYM SALOMON

[1740(?)–1785]

by *Virginius Dabney*

H AYM SALOMON, Polish-born American patriot, rendered important services to the revolutionary cause at the risk of his life, and at great financial sacrifice.

An advocate of Polish liberty, he fled from his native land on the eve of the Revolution and came to New York. Entering the brokerage and commission merchant's business in the American city, he was highly successful.

Upon the outbreak of hostilities with the British, Salomon was ardently sympathetic to the Revolution. When the British occupied New York, he was arrested. During his imprisonment he sought to persuade Hessian soldiers to desert, and is said to have aided French and American prisoners to escape. He was released but was again marked for arrest by the British, and managed to flee to the American lines, leaving behind his family and all his possessions. In a petition to the Continental Congress in Philadelphia, dated August 25, 1778, Salomon declared concerning his escape:

> Your Memorialist had upon this Event irrevocably lost all his Effects and Credits to the Amount of five or six thousand Pounds sterling and left his distressed Wife and Child of a Month old at New York waiting that they may have an Opportunity to come out from thence with empty hands.
>
> In these Circumstances he most humbly prayeth to grant him any

[211]

Employ in the Way of his Business whereby he may be enabled to support himself and family.

Salomon's petition to the Congress did not result in any employment. With the assistance of friends, he managed to get himself established in Philadelphia as a dealer in bills of exchange and other securities. His wife and child joined him, and in a few years he became financially secure again.

Salomon used his financial resources to aid the patriot cause, in association with Robert Morris. He did not lend or give vast sums to the struggling Continentals, as has sometimes been claimed, but acted as a broker for securities of the bankrupt government and helped to shore up its credit. He lent money, without interest, to financially strapped members of Congress, and made it possible for them to remain in Philadelphia. Among those thus assisted were James Madison, Edmund Randolph, and a number of Pennsylvanians.

Oscar Handlin, the historian, has written of Salomon's role in the Revolution: "Others held back and hesitated, but this American, though less than a decade in the country, had never a doubt."

In 1781 and 1782 he sold about $200,000 worth of government securities and received a broker's fee. But following his death in 1785, aged about forty-five, the settlement of his estate showed assets, including revolutionary securities, valued at $44,732 against indebtedness of $45,292. Thus he died insolvent.

Researches by Samuel Oppenheim, Max Kohler, and Jacob Marcus into Salomon's career have given us a clearer picture of his services, and at the same time have exploded various myths, including one that he was condemned to death by the British. Enough remains for us to regard him as a leading patriot of the American Revolution.

HAYM SALOMON

Sculpture designed by
Lorado Taft

[THE PATRIOTIC FOUNDATION OF CHICAGO]

PHILIP JOHN SCHUYLER

[1733–1804]

by *William F. Buckley, Jr.*

"[S C H U Y L E R A N D I] got into a little contest," wrote Jefferson to Madison in 1792, "whether hereditary descent or election was most likely to bring *wise* and *honest* men into public councils. He for the former . . . myself for the latter." The career of Philip John Schuyler (1733–1804), gentleman and general, helps explain why sans-culottism remained—and remains—foreign to the American tradition. It was altogether appropriate that Schuyler should have obtained the services of Edmund Burke as New York's English agent, even if his motive was political rather than philosophical. Appropriate, too, was his close relationship to Alexander Hamilton, whose marriage to Schuyler's daughter Elizabeth cemented paternal and temperamental affinities.

Schuyler is remembered as a revolutionary major general. Overcoming awesome difficulties, he helped to achieve the victory at Saratoga, essential to the success of the Revolution. He was had up, by old enemies, on scurrilous charges but was vindicated by a military court of honor. He nevertheless resigned his commission, but stayed on as Washington's advisor on Indian affairs, from which cockpit he contrived the cooperation with French arms that led, ultimately, to Yorktown.

Textbooks record his military accomplishments. Schuyler was more interesting, and more significant, as the prototypical patrician-patriot. Schuyler, the fourth generation New Yorker, was an entirely different New Man from Crèvecoeur's. Schuyler was a genuine American aristocrat. Proud, ambitious, practical, scholarly (he mastered five languages and corresponded with Rittenhouse on the mathematics of astronomy), Schuyler led the patriot cause in the New York Assembly. But he led the cause in order to moderate its excesses. The new state's first constitution, which he helped draft, guaranteed that New York's would not be a Jacobinical revolution.

From his seat in the new state senate, he labored to curb the "democratical" proclivities of the states by a strengthened national government. A senator in the first sitting of the federal legislature, Schuyler firmly supported Hamilton's fiscal program. In state and national office, Schuyler embodied a Federalism that deplored "the destructive principles which prevail in France." Humanitarian (he led in prison reform), visionary (he helped create an inland waterway system that eventuated in the Erie Canal), philanthropist (a regent of the State University, he also was a founder of Union College, Schenectady), this patrician republican was the embodiment of that ordered liberty which is the true legacy of the American Revolution.

PHILIP SCHUYLER

by John Trumbull

[THE NEW YORK HISTORICAL SOCIETY]

ROGER SHERMAN

[1721–1793]

by Clifford K. Shipton

R OGER SHERMAN (1721–93) was born in Massachusetts and had his primary education in its public schools. He then came under the influence of the Reverend Samuel Dunbar, from whom he acquired the essentials of a liberal, practical, and theological education. Having then learned the cobbler's trade, he took his tools on his back and walked to New Milford, Connecticut. Two years later he became the county surveyor, and quickly worked his way through the town and church offices, at the same time becoming a substantial merchant and the publisher of a very successful literary almanac. Brushing up on the law, he was elected to the legislature and sent to Albany to serve as commissary during the French and Indian War. After it, he was appointed to the Superior Court of Connecticut, on which he served for twenty-three years.

Sherman took the advanced view in 1774 that the British Parliament "had authority to make laws for America in no case whatever." He expressed this opinion "heavily and clumsily" as a member of the Continental Congress, a body in which he served from its inception until 1781, and then in 1783 and 1784. Despite his lack of eloquence, his influence in the Congress was unsurpassed. Sherman was a member of the committee to draft the Declaration of Independence, as well as numerous other committees, and he worked indefatigably. John Adams referred to him as "an old Puritan, as honest as an angel and as firm in the cause of American Independence as Mount Atlas."

When the Revolution broke out, he moved against the lawless violence of the mobs, but his attitude was determined by the fact that he was a chief magistrate of what had been for all practical purposes an independent republic for more than a century.

Sherman affixed his signature to the Declaration of Independence and supported a strong financial policy and the federal union. Although he opposed the democratic tendency of the Constitution, he signed that document and campaigned strongly for ratification. His series of letters "To the People of Connecticut," published in the *New Haven Gazette* over the pseudonym "A Countryman," was influential in creating a favorable opinion in that state.

Sherman had the distinction of being the only person to sign the Articles of Association of 1774, the Declaration of Independence, the Articles of Confederation, and the Constitution of the United States.

Elected to the House in the First Congress and then (1791) to the Senate, he showed in his political attitude some of the less desirable qualities of puritanism. Yet no one could question the industry, integrity, and Yankee common sense of his public service.

ROGER SHERMAN

by Ralph Earl

[YALE UNIVERSITY ART GALLERY]

GILBERT STUART

[1755–1828]

by James Thomas Flexner

A MONG ALL American portrait painters, Gilbert Stuart and John Singer Sargent had the most suave techniques. But where Sargent was also flattering in the images he produced, Stuart was not. Sargent typically showed his sitters as admirable examples of social privilege. But Stuart belonged to the generation of the American Revolution. It was, he said, the portrait painter's duty to ignore rank and wealth, to put down exactly "the animal" before him.

Stuart's father had been brought from Scotland to erect New England's "first engine for the manufacture of snuff." The painter was born in Rhode Island during 1755. At the age of five, he drew on the earth with a stick a "perfect likeness of a neighbor." Soon he was leading on the streets of Newport a gang of urchins engaged in outrageous pranks.

Stuart was apprenticed at an early age to a visiting artist, Cosmo Alexander, whom he accompanied back to Scotland. When Alexander died, the boy was left in destitution; he worked his way home before the mast. Since he had studied abroad, the Rhode Island provincials eagerly sat to him for portraits. It developed that the lad had refused to abandon, for the conventional graces Alexander had practiced, the strong but crabbed style of an American vernacular artist.

Stuart's parents were Tories; they fled the Revolution to Halifax. The youth sailed for London where, still refusing all sophisticated influences, he tried to sell portraits painted in his crude American style. Only utter failure made him look around him. Then with sensational speed he mastered the techniques of what was then Europe's most accomplished portrait school. Upper-middle-class connois-

[223]

seurs soon expressed the belief that he would succeed those aging academicians, Reynolds and Gainsborough, as the leader of British portraiture. However, social and artistic conservatives insisted that his likenesses lacked elegance; he merely "nailed the face to the canvas."

Success made Stuart more dissipated and extravagant. He was forced to flee his debts, first to Ireland and then to America. Reaching New York in 1792 or 1793, he instantly overwhelmed the American public. It seemed to his fellow artist, William Dunlap, as if "I had never seen portraits before, so decidedly was form and mind portrayed."

To make his living in Great Britain, Stuart had often been forced to compromise by surrounding his shrewd likenesses with accessories indicative of rank. Back home in individualistic America, he was free to subordinate everything to the face. Often he showed nothing but a head placed, with the minimum of body needed to give it position, against a plain background. These were social-revolutionary pictures, since they assumed that an individual's worth was in himself, in his own character, irrespective of any worldly circumstance.

Stuart depicted a broad spectrum of the men who had led the Revolution and of the women who had assisted them. As everyone knows, he painted Washington. In the presence of the hero the weak side of the artist's self-reliance came out. He held it against Washington that he allowed himself to be persuaded by American conservatives to paint elaborate full-lengths of the president that violated his own social and artistic ideals. Even when he put Washington's head in all simplicity on an unadorned canvas (as he did in some of his best-known *Washingtons*) he could not forgive that this was a great man viewed by the world with reverence. In self-protective rage, he would dwell so strongly on Washington's misshapen mouth that the pictures have encouraged iconoclasts to think of the father of our country primarily as an old man with ill-fitting false teeth.

Stuart remained an effective artist until he died in 1828 at the age of seventy-two. We must look beyond his *Washingtons* to realize his brilliance as a painter and how much the United States owes him for preserving the appearance and character of so many of our founders.

GILBERT STUART

by Rembrandt Peale and Charles Willson Peale

JOHN TRUMBULL

[1756–1843]

by *Charles Coleman Sellers*

T HE KEYNOTE in the long life (1756–1843) of "The Artist of the Revolution" is pride—a sensitive, aggressive pride in social and military rank, in his profession, in his country. He was the youngest son of Governor Jonathan Trumbull of Connecticut, "Brother Jonathan" of those days, and had grown up as a sickly child, blinded in one eye at the age of four. In boyhood, nonetheless, it became his fixed ambition to become an artist—and a great artist, for only great artists ranked as gentlemen. It overrode kindly but firm parental opposition.

He graduated from Harvard in 1773, youngest in his class, and two years later at the outbreak of war, his father secured him a commission as adjutant in the First Connecticut Regiment, marching to the siege of Boston. At Cambridge, his accurately drawn maps caught the eye of General Washington, who placed him on his staff with the rank of lieutenant colonel. He rendered good service in the siege, but sought a more active role and became adjutant general under Horatio Gates at Crown Point and Ticonderoga, then saw service with General Benedict Arnold in Rhode Island, wintering at Providence. There, April 17, 1777, receiving his colonel's commission from Congress and finding it dated three months later than expected, he immediately resigned from the army and retired to Boston to study art—until the fighting in Rhode Island in the summer of 1778 brought him back as a volunteer on General Sullivan's staff, a brief but dashing and effective service under fire.

Again he was in Boston, where his only resource in art study was the collection of paintings brought to America years before by John Smibert. By special arrangement in high quarters, the way was cleared for a move to London and the studio of Benjamin West. Here, November 19, 1780, he was suddenly arrested on "suspicion of high treason." It was an act of reprisal for the hanging of Major John André, to whom Trumbull could be seen as a very near equivalent should the authorities choose an American to suffer the same fate. West interceded with the king, who gave his promise that, whatever the verdict of the courts, the young man's life would be safe. Released at last without trial, Trumbull left for the Continent, not returning until after the peace.

Once again with West, he took up the project which West had conceived, but could not appropriately continue while employed as historical painter to the king—a series of major paintings celebrating events of the war and the final victory. To this, his "National Work," the remainder of Trumbull's life was very largely dedicated, composing the scenes, studying the sites, and traveling through America to obtain portraits of the actors in them. The originals would be published as engravings, bringing them to the public at large and insuring a supporting income.

The first were the most vivid and spirited, *The Battle of Bunker Hill* and *The Death of General Montgomery at Quebec*. Then came *The Surrender of Cornwallis*, *The Death of General Mercer at Princeton*, *The Capture of the Hessians at Trenton*, and *The Declaration of Independence*, with thirty-six of his forty-eight portraits painted from life. In 1818, his *Surrender of Burgoyne*, *Surrender of Cornwallis*, *Declaration of Independence*, and *Resignation of Washington at Annapolis* were painted in large size for the Rotunda of the Capitol, crowning the whole of this long effort.

In the meantime he had served his country in diplomatic missions, engaged in some commercial ventures, and through it all built up an oeuvre of portraits and landscapes. In his latter years, active in New York, he would long be remembered as the "Old Colonel," handsome, punctilious, impetuous, stern. As president of the American Academy of Fine Arts he maintained standards that won him no popularity with the younger artists. In 1831, he assigned all the works in his studio to Yale in return for an annuity—America's first college museum of art. There they remain and there he himself lies buried. It is the personal monument of one who had given, in his own words, "my Sword and Pencil to my Country."

JOHN TRUMBULL

by Samuel Lovett Waldo and William Jewett

[YALE UNIVERSITY ART GALLERY]

MERCY OTIS WARREN

[1728–1814]

by *John J. Waters*

M ERCY OTIS WARREN, the patriot, feminist, and author, believed that the "faithful historian delineates characters truly, let the censure fall where it will." Her insightful letters, her satirical sketches, and her boldness in attacking John Adams, the former Federalist and president, show that she practiced what she preached. Mercy (born on Cape Cod in 1728) was the first daughter of James Otis, Sr., a traditional provincial politician. She learned the basic literary skills from her Uncle Russell, minister of the Barnstable Church, who through his books opened up to her vistas of the larger world. However, once Mercy could read and write she was forced into ladylike needlework while she enviously watched her brother James perfect his Latin and Greek. All of this she intensely resented and wrote that if females dealt with trifles, and men with power the "deficiency lies not so much in [the] inferiour contexture of female intellects as in the different education bestowed on the sexes."

Marriages in the Otis family, as well as all career decisions, reflected the "patriarchship"—Mercy's own word for her father as an institution—who used his children as pieces in the chess game of power. Thus in 1754 Mercy married James Warren, scion of a distinguished Plymouth family, son of an ally of her father, and college friend of her favorite brother James. With her husband she shared a formally correct marriage and mothered five children. James Warren, less gifted and ambitious than his wife, realized her strength and said in an intended compliment that she had a "woman's temperament but a man's mind." In bringing up her own children she rejected the "irksome methods of severity" that had marked her own childhood and favored greater liberty. Mercy chafed under the "narrow bounds" of the required female role even while she rationalized that women should accept the "appointed subordination" of the marriage state not because they are really subordinate but rather "for the sake of order in families."

Mercy Otis Warren saw in the patriot struggle against Great Britain reflections of her own fight for an identity. She was first helped in this by her brother James Otis, Jr., who made her his confidante and assured her that "no man ever loved a sister better." Mercy, in turn, acted as his mediator before the "God of Heaven" and told him that he remained the "continual subject of both my sleeping and waking thoughts." Yet she realized that she needed a larger audience than her family. When she took pen in hand she faced the world and the future. Mercy knew that this was a bold and assertive act for a female but then she held that the American Revolution revealed the hand of Providence and the unfolding in time of the spirit of "universal liberty." In her play *The Group* (1775) she cast her brother as Brutus and all her patriots are "Resolved to die or see their country free." Mercy Otis Warren caught the temper of radical Boston with its protests against corrupt tax officials, police searches, British officeholders, and its resentment of the Hutchinson-Oliver "monopoly" of political jobs. Nor did the death of her brother in 1783 or family difficulties still her opinion that her generation partook in the "foundation of that glorious revolution which will be considered among the most interesting events in the annals of time."

In 1805 Mercy Warren, having championed the French Revolution and favored the Jeffersonian Republicans in Federalist Boston, published her unique three-volume *History of the Rise, Progress and Termination of the American Revolution*. Ever the democrat, she presented the thesis that revolutions are the "sudden rotations in human affairs . . . permitted by Providence, to remind mankind of their natural equality, to check the pride of wealth, to restrain the insolence of rank and family distinctions, which too frequently oppress the various classes in society." Until her death in 1814 she engaged in polemics, giving as she took. Mercy Otis Warren knew that she was not loved, but by her writings she ensured that she would be remembered in her own words.

MERCY WARREN

by John Singleton Copley

[MUSEUM OF FINE ARTS, BOSTON]

MARTHA WASHINGTON

[1731–1802]

by James Thomas Flexner

WHEN PRESIDENT WASHINGTON was embattled with the Jeffersonians, Albert Gallatin, who was to be Jefferson's secretary of the treasury, described Mrs. Washington as "a very good natured and amiable woman. Not so," Gallatin contended, "her husband." The most amazing thing about Martha Washington was that during her long life, at home and in the conspicuous stations she occupied, she charmed everyone she met, never made an enemy.

Born Martha Dandridge to a simple Virginia family, she was carried by her ability to soothe into wealth and position. Daniel Parke Custis had been unable to get married because his cantankerous father had repudiated every possible bride. But Martha charmed the tyrant, becoming at eighteen the wife of the thirty-seven-year-old Daniel. When, eight years later, he left her a widow, she was, due to his estate, one of the richest marriageable women in Virginia.

The plump, diminutive lady—she was hardly five feet tall—became the bride of Virginia's tremendous—Washington was more than six feet—French and Indian War hero. The match was for him in part a marriage of convenience. He was trying to disentangle himself from a married woman he loved, and Martha's wealth raised him into the first rank of Virginia planters. There was trouble between the couple at first, but Martha's human gifts again triumphed. Washington soon stated that marriage was the most important event in life, the most conducive to misery or happiness.

One of George Washington's greatest contributions to the revolutionary victory was the steadfastness that helped him to keep, despite all discouragements, an army ever in the field. For eight years, he never took one day of furlough. Perhaps even as strong a man as he could not have borne the strain had not Martha supported him and the cause by "marching" (as he put it) every year to whatever headquarters her husband occupied during the winter's pause in the fighting. She felt compelled to leave behind, however reluctantly, the gentleness of Mount Vernon, because "the poor general was so unhappy that it distressed me exceedingly." With her doing fine needlework beside him he could, as the snow fell outside, almost forget the war. Bringing with her always "domestic felicity," the comfort of the hearth, Martha made—as she was again to do when Washington was president—a profound contribution to the creation of the United States.

However, she had no desire to interfere in great affairs or flash as a great belle. And her husband had enough of excitement away from her side. She brought him always the comfort of the hearth. She was the only human being whom he allowed to penetrate to the soft inner core of his nature, where dwelt that diffidence and extreme sensitivity which manifested itself on the surface in his excruciating vulnerability to criticism.

The Washington marriage was childless, but Martha had children and grandchildren from her previous marriage. For them she was overprotective, shielding them even from her powerful husband. For the rest, her life was wrapped up in his. Resentful always of the interference of the outside world, determined to keep something to herself at last, she burned, after her husband's death, all their correspondence with each other.

MARTHA WASHINGTON

by Charles Willson Peale

[INDEPENDENCE NATIONAL HISTORICAL PARK COLLECTION, PHILADELPHIA]

"MAD" ANTHONY WAYNE

[1745–1796]

by Jenkin Lloyd Jones

THEY CALLED HIM MAD when he ordered the starved and ragged relics of the American disaster at Quebec to appear on the Ticonderoga parade ground with their hair powdered and plaited.

But how better can you rebuild the spirits of the spiritless than by the appearance of polish and pride?

They called him mad when he ordered Stony Point taken by cold steel and threatened to kill the first man who fired a shot.

But in a night so black that only cockades of white paper distinguished friend from foe what good would musket fire have been in the rush across the parapets?

And at Green Spring on the James River when his Pennsylvania line fell into Cornwallis's trap and faced annihilation it seemed a mad thing to order a great drum-beating, trumpet-blowing assault by 800 against 5,000.

But how else could Cornwallis have been induced to snap open the trap and withdraw, fearing that the whole American army had come up?

So he wasn't mad, after all. Not Anthony Wayne, the gentleman farmer of Waynesboro, Pennsylvania, grown out of a boy who had paraded in the fields with a shouldered stick.

He was an uncomplicated man, a limited man. He could hardly follow the philosophical arguments of Jefferson and Hamilton. He loved war. But in an age when it was common to put fortress defenders to the sword he was quick with quarter.

He could understand the value of the waiting game and the wisdom of retreat. But at interminable high command debates in which the timid and irresolute often prevailed he would sit in a corner, muttering, "I say we fight!"

At a time when some men felt light loyalties to the fledgling nation, when Charles Lee apparently played the British game at Monmouth, when Benedict Arnold defected, when the Conway Cabal spread dissension in the camps, there was never any question about Wayne. He was a team player.

But, most important, he was a soldier who stayed—stayed after Yorktown, after the flags had been taken and the bands had gone home.

Washington sent him to Georgia to allay the nightmare of revenge that shook the former Tories. And when the incompetent General St. Clair almost lost the Ohio frontier to the rampaging Six Nations it was Wayne who trained a new army. For the first time it began to dawn on some Americans that nationhood implied continuing obligations.

At Fallen Timbers in 1794 he broke the Indian Confederation and ended the influence of the British over the western tribes. Wayne's unspeakable second in command, General James Wilkinson, his pockets lined with Spanish gold, could no longer undermine him. He built Fort Wayne, and after that admirers and old comrades turned out Waynesvilles, Waynesburgs, and Wayne Counties in profusion.

Aged fifty-two, the widower received the surrender of Detroit and hurried east to marry the lovely Mary Vining. Complications, stemming from a wound that had been, oddly enough, inflicted fifteen years before by an excitable French sentry at Yorktown, caught up with him at Erie. There was a brief twilight.

"Bury me on the hill beside the flag," he said.

ANTHONY WAYNE

by John Trumbull

NOAH WEBSTER

[1758–1843]

by Henry Steele Commager

EVEN AS THE American ministers in France were putting their names to the treaty that acknowledged the political independence of America from the mother country, a young schoolteacher up in Goshen, New York, was preparing what was to be a cultural and linguistic declaration of independence. The book, published (at his own expense) in the spring of 1783 with the pretentious title *A Grammatical Institute of the English Language, Part I* was renamed, in the next edition, *An American Spelling Book;* to generations of American children it was simply known as Webster's *Blue Backed Speller*. It caught on; soon it monopolized the field; under its benign guidance millions of American children learned the same words, the same spelling, the same pronunciation; read the same stories; absorbed the same moral lessons. Already at the age of twenty-five Webster was launched upon his career as Schoolmaster of America.

But he was more than this, far more. He was one of the Founding Fathers of American nationalism; more effectively than any other man of his time he laid the foundations for that cultural unity so essential to harmonious nationalism.

Noah Webster was very conscious of his mission; indeed in time he came to think that he was divinely ordained to fulfill it. "America," he wrote, "must be independent in literature as she is in politics." And he admonished his countrymen to "unshackle your minds. You have an empire to raise and support by your exertions and a national character to establish and extend by your wisdom and virtue."

The speller—which sold eventually some sixty million copies—and after it a long series of spellers, readers, and dictionaries, made Webster the guiding spirit in the enterprise of cultural nationalism in young America. Over the years he consolidated and extended that position. Wherever we look there is Noah Webster, dour, angular, and aggressive, busily fathering institutions we now think of as characteristically American. He was the father of the American language; he was one of the fathers of American education. If we turn to that group of statesmen who made the Constitution, there is Webster holding aloft his *Sketches of American Policy*. He is one of the contributors, too, to American political philosophy, for in voluminous pages he told Hamilton how to run the economy and the Federalist party, Madison how to conduct the presidency, and he instructed Jefferson on the nature of American democracy. If we look to journalism there is Webster, editor of the *American Magazine* and of several newspapers, too. If we consider science, there too is Webster, edging up on Dr. Franklin and Dr. Rush, hopefully proffering us his two-volume *History of Epidemics*, and with scientific articles bulging in his coat pockets. He is the father of American copyright, assisted at the birth of the census, and with his many school histories and readers is—perhaps with Parson Weems—one of the fathers of American history, while his many essays on banking, finance, insurance, and public policy support his claim to be a pioneer in the American economy. And finally his singlehanded revision of the Bible—he thought this his greatest work—permits us to call him one of the fathers of the church.

In the end it is to his speller and his dictionary that he owes his immortality. The dictionary, which appeared first in 1806 and then—monumentally—in 1828, achieved the distinction of being an institution in itself, and still flourishes. The speller conquered the land. It was born in New England; it went west with the Conestoga wagon; it leaped the continent and established its empire on the Pacific coast; it even invaded the South, and it was no other than Jefferson Davis who said, on the eve of secession, that "above all books which have united us in the bond of common language, I place the good old Spelling Book of Noah Webster." In the whole of our history no other secular book has ever spread so wide, penetrated so deep, or lasted so long.

NOAH WEBSTER

by James Sharples, Sr.

GEORGE WYTHE

[1726–1806]

by *Virginius Dabney*

G EORGE WYTHE, signer of the Declaration of Independence, was one of the few American leaders who took the advanced position before the outbreak of hostilities in the Revolution that Great Britain had no more authority over us than we had over Great Britain. He was also one of the greatest jurists and teachers this country has produced. Thomas Jefferson, John Marshall, and Henry Clay were his law students.

Jefferson wrote of Wythe that "on the first dawn" of the American Revolution, "instead of higgling on half-way principles, as others did who feared to follow their reason, he took his stand on the solid ground that the only link of political union between us and Great Britain was the identity of our executive; that that nation and its Parliament had no more authority over us than we had over them, and that we were coordinate nations with Great Britain and Hanover."

Wythe, who had been born on his father's plantation in Elizabeth City County, Virginia, in 1726, served several terms in the Virginia House of Burgesses, rising to the post of speaker. He was elected a member of the Continental Congress in 1775, and the following year signed the Declaration of Independence at the head of the Virginia delegation.

In 1778 he became one of the three judges of the new Virginia High Court of Chancery, and the following year was named professor of law and police at the College of William and Mary, the first chair of its kind in this country.

Wythe served briefly in 1787 at the Philadelphia convention that framed the federal Constitution. He also served throughout the Virginia Constitutional Convention which met the following year and ratified that document by a narrow margin. Wythe presided several times when the Virginia convention went into the Committee of the Whole, and he made the motion for ratification.

In 1789 Wythe moved to Richmond from Williamsburg, where he had lived in a house that is one of today's show places. His removal to Richmond, which had been chosen the capital some years before, was deemed desirable because he had been named chancellor of Virginia upon the reorganization of the state's judicial system.

Chancellor Wythe lived there for seventeen years in a much less pretentious house than he had occupied in Williamsburg, for he had come to Richmond at considerable financial sacrifice. The town was shocked in 1806 when, at age eighty, he was murdered by his grandnephew, George Wythe Sweeney, who put arsenic in his morning coffee. The old man lingered in agony for two weeks. Sweeney's motive is supposed to have been a desire to acquire his inheritance from his granduncle at once, since he was in serious financial trouble. Wythe lived long enough to grasp what had happened, and to disinherit Sweeney. He was buried in the churchyard of old St. John's, where in 1775 Patrick Henry had called for "liberty or death."

George Wythe was one of the most beloved and admired men of the age. Said to be "the best Latin and Greek scholar in the State," he was also a superlative teacher of the law. His students revered him. As a jurist he was often compared to Aristides "the Just." Unusually gracious in manner, Henry Clay said that "he made the most graceful bow I ever witnessed." Jefferson termed him "the honor of his own and the model for future times."

GEORGE WYTHE

by *William Crossman*

[COLONIAL WILLIAMSBURG]